INDIA

GOOD STORIES REVEAL as much, or more, about a locale as any map or guidebook. Whereabouts Press is dedicated to publishing books that will enlighten a traveler to the soul of a place. By bringing a country's stories to the English-speaking reader, we hope to convey its culture through literature. Books from Whereabouts Press are essential companions for the curious traveler, and for the person who appreciates how fine writing enhances one's experiences in the world.

"Coming newly into Spanish, I lacked two essentials—a childhood in the language, which I could never acquire, and a sense of its literature, which I could."

—Alastair Reid, *Whereabouts:*
Notes on Being a Foreigner

OTHER TRAVELER'S LITERARY COMPANIONS

Amsterdam	*Ireland*
Argentina	*Israel*
Australia	*Italy*
Brazil	*Japan*
Chile	*Mexico*
China	*Prague*
Costa Rica	*South Africa*
Cuba	*Spain*
France	*Vienna*
Greece	*Vietnam*

INDIA

A TRAVELER'S LITERARY COMPANION

EDITED BY

CHANDRAHAS CHOUDHURY

FOREWORD BY

ANITA DESAI

WHEREABOUTS PRESS
BERKELEY, CALIFORNIA

Copyright © 2010 by Whereabouts Press

Preface © 2010 by Chandrahas Choudhury
Foreword © 2010 by Anita Desai
(complete copyright information on page 233)

Map of India by BookMatters

Published by
Whereabouts Press
Berkeley, California
www.whereaboutspress.com

Distributed to the trade by PGW / Perseus Distribution

MANUFACTURED IN THE UNITED STATES OF AMERICA

Library of Congress Cataloging-in-Publication Data

India : a traveler's literary companion /
edited by Chandrahas Choudhury ;
foreword by Anita Desai.
p.   cm.
About half the stories were written in English,
and the other half are translations,
each from a different Indian language.
ISBN 978-1-883513-24-5 (alk. paper)
1. India—Fiction.
2. Short stories, India (English)
3. Short stories, India.
4. Short stories, India—Translations into English.
5. India fiction—20th century.
I. Choudhury, Chandrahas.
PR9497.32.I49   2010
809.3'935854—DC22
2010014338

5 4 3 2 1

Contents

Foreword

Anita Desai

The premise for this collection is both curious and original. The fiction brought together between the covers of this book has been charged with presenting geographical location. This is generally the purpose of "travel writing" and it is to that, or to "nature writing," that we turn when we want landscape—or any space—made visible to us. Fiction may do this but not necessarily. Instead of landscape, it is characters, their speech, thoughts, and actions that take precedence, the landscape providing a backdrop like a set in the theatre. Rarely does the set engage us above the sounds and actions produced by the figures on stage. Rather, it provides us with suggestions regarding the background of the characters and their actions. And in theatre it can even be dispensed with altogether and the play may still produce the required effect if the script and the actors are powerful and evocative enough.

So it is, too, in fiction. There are stories in which the background is a powerful presence in itself, even an inextricable part of the narrative, and there are stories that dispense with it in favour of the other elements of story.

But here we have a collection of stories that will present, we are told, audaciously: India. So the reader is turned into a traveler, and the book being read into a "companion." Do these stories fulfill this goal? When the subject is India, one would think such an enterprise is so daunting as to appear almost impossible, for India is not only a country made up of so many different ecosystems—easy enough to convey—but of so many languages, each with its own tone and rhythm, so many flavours, so many religious and cultural specificities, that to impose any coherence or convergence upon them is somehow to falsify them.

Fortunately, the writers of these stories were given no such intimidating instructions. They were all writing the short stories and novels that they wished to write, the ones that grew out of their own experiences and perceptions of their worlds. So their spontaneity is intact—very important, this—and they do not convey any impression that the writers laboured to produce a portrait of a certain geographical area. Instead, they engage with characters, their speech and actions, just as any writer of fiction does; and the geographical area, along with its social, linguistic, and cultural distinctions, evolves naturally out of the narrative.

The stories are categorized according to the regions in which they are set, regions which share some broad commonalities—the north, the south, the east, and west, and India's often-neglected northeast—and, in presenting the lives lived in these areas in all their disorderly, discordant, irrepressible variety, also initiate the reader into an appreciation of both nature and culture in their many Indian forms.

In the stories we have from the north, Qurratulain Hyder writes of the social snobberies created by a shifting social structure in an urban environment where everyone is trying to outdo the others, and Kunal Basu portrays an office worker who creates for himself a richer world of his imagination. From the east we have two stories that are set in a world so rural and isolated as to seem to belong to the remote past, but a third, by Bibhutibhushan Bandhopadhyay, is filled with the hustle-bustle of urban lives. In the northeast, the characters created by Mamang Dai have a more spacious natural world in which to breathe, and the landscape is a presence in itself. From the west, we have one story that is rich with the labour and the hazards of the sea and seafarers' lives, another that presents the seaside as a pleasure resort for idle lives, and a third tale that is harsh with the melodrama of criminal acts and criminal minds. The south too yields stories with totally different moods and intentions: one a kind of picaresque, another a portrait of a very traditional society, and a third of a misfit and outsider to all tradition.

Composed at different times over the last hundred years and teeming with the kind of local detail that is the mark of a sensibility that loves a city, a village, a landscape, and sees in it the whole world, these stories by diverse hands are a kaleidoscope of the traditional and modern, the urban and the rural, the wealthy and the impoverished—a revealing glimpse into the many Indias encompassed by that fathomless word "India."

Anita Desai
February 2010

Preface

Much of the pleasure of storytelling comes from all that is left unsaid—from the things for which we readers are given a direction, but not an end. So too, so much of what we feel for the world of a story derives from the flavour of the local—from a turn of phrase, a glimpse of a patch of earth, a memorable detail, that is absolutely specific to the worldview of a particular character or culture.

When, for instance, Chandrakant, the youth leaving his village for the first time in Jayant Kaikini's story "Dots and Lines," feels the wind on his face on the train to Bombay and imagines that the same wind "had just blown the tarpaulin off the night-halting bus on the banks of the Gangavati before reaching this place," this image makes us see Chandrakant in two places at the same time. Not only does the idea of the wind from home catching up with the train going away from home encapsulate Chandrakant's longing for what he has left behind, the specificity of the image of "the tarpaulin of the night-halting bus" being ruffled by that wind registers very strongly on our own imaginations: it is one of those flares of detail that make fiction burn brighter than other kinds of prose writing.

Similarly, in Bibhutibhushan Bandhopadhyay's "Canvasser Krishnalal," we are told of Krishnalal, the itinerant seller of medicated oil, that "he would ply like a weaver's shuttle, from Shiyalda to Barasat, from Barasat to Shiyalda." This detail not only makes Krishnalal seem like a mechanised object himself, operating upon the world with the same regularity and constancy as that of a season or the trains, it also suggests the man's jaunty temperament—it might be a metaphor thought of by Krishnalal himself. We understand, from such details, why Eudora Welty thought that while fiction's reach, its themes, were universal, the power of a story was "all bound up in the local."

This anthology brings to you a basket of such stories, plucked out of the gardens of literature from India's many languages: works that are intended to bring you closer to the Indian landscape and the Indian imagination in all its variety, even as you enjoy the universal pleasures of storytelling. About half the stories here were written in English, and the other half are translations, each from a different Indian language. Indeed, the most striking feature of Indian literature when seen as a whole—a source of its strength and variety, but also of the difficulty in navigating it—is that it is multilingual to a degree not matched by any other national literature in the world. Even if we exclude classical languages and contemporary dialects, we find ourselves before a field divided up among at least two dozen languages. As with any other language, each one of these languages represents not only a particular matrix of sounds and grammatical structures but also a distinct imaginative universe, with its own myths and beliefs, its own social structures, its own view of history and time.

Thus we arrive at the paradox: because of its profusion of languages, most of Indian literature is a foreign country even for Indian readers, who at their best can be no more than trilingual or quadrilingual. I myself speak English, Hindi—which is the closest that India has to a "national" language—and my mother tongue Oriya, and, I am ashamed to admit, can only read and write in the first two, although I can sing you a number of devotional songs in the third.

Unsurprisingly, as English is the language of university education and also the favoured language of the Indian elite, a link language between people whose first languages are different from each other, and also the language that links India to the world, it is Indian writing in English—a realm in which much exciting work is being done—that receives the most attention both at home and around the world. Another factor inhibiting the appreciation of the literature from other Indian languages has been the paucity of good translations into English. These are the conditions that led Salman Rushdie and Elizabeth West to controversially declare, in their 1997 anthology *Mirrorwork: 50 Years of Indian Writing 1947-1997*, that "the prose writing . . . created in this period by Indian writers *working in English*, is proving to be a stronger and more important body of work that most of what has been produced in the 16 'official languages' of India," and that "'Indo-Anglian' literature represents perhaps the most valuable contribution India has yet made to the world of books."

This is a contention—as I hope this book will demonstrate—that is being disproved rapidly. But the point remains: many of the riches of Indian literature are lying invisible in the shadows, waiting for a translation that will release their rhythms and energies into the world. It is my hope that some of the stories in this volume showcase the best of what is currently available of Indian fiction in English translation, and arouse in you, the reader interested in India, the desire for a more sustained encounter with writers whose work is every bit as good as their better-known counterparts who compose in English.

As with other anthologies in this series, the stories here are arranged on a geographical basis, almost laid out on a map. Each of the five regions in which I have divided the country could potentially have been the subject of an individual book, but here I have limited them to two or three stories each. Where the stories are set in a specific city or town, those have been named; otherwise the general region or state in which the story is set has been provided. I have tried to make sure that the book gives a sense of the different realities of urban, small-town, and rural India, from the world of upper-class Delhi represented in Qurratulain Hyder's "The Sound of Falling Leaves" to the village people gossiping and squabbling by the pond in Fakir Mohan Senapati's "Asura Pond." The stories also gesture at the diverse primary allegiances of Indian people, whether it is to the city (Bandhopadhyay's Krishnalal), the guild (Nazir Mansuri's fisherman, Lakham Patari), caste (Phanishwarnath Renu's villagers), or the tribe (Mamang Dai's heroine, Nenem). The works brought together here are both old and new: the earliest was first published in 1902, while the ink is still not dry on the most recent one. Some of the writers here are legendary figures known to, even if not always read by, readers all over India; others represent the new generation, and are slowly making a reputation for themselves. I have made some notes on aspects of their craft and style in the individual introductions to the stories.

Not the least of the pleasures of the stories brought together here is that, while rooted in a particular world, they often hum with the stirrings of distant worlds that have made India such a diverse and fecund civilization. The architect of the Taj Mahal in Kunal Basu's "The Accountant" looks at an architectural plan "drawn not simply from Hindustan but from Isphafan and Constantinople, Kabul and Samarkand—from the whole world." In Nazir Mansuri's "The Whale," a trader in a port village on the west coast of India ferries "lime, dates, onions, and garlic to Basra, Iran, and Africa" till one day he never returns. Now these stories, too, go out into the world— many of them are being published outside India for the first time—and it is my hope that wherever they go, they will provide the same pleasure that they have given at home.

Chandrahas Choudhury
Mumbai, March 2010

The Prophet's Hair

Salman Rushdie

EARLY IN THE YEAR 19-, when Srinagar was under the spell of a winter so fierce it could crack men's bones as if they were glass, a young man upon whose cold-pinked skin there lay, like a frost, the unmistakable sheen of wealth was to be seen entering the most wretched and disreputable part of the city, where the houses of wood and corrugated iron seemed perpetually on the verge of

SALMAN RUSHDIE (1947–) is the author, most notably, of *Midnight's Children* (1981), *The Satanic Verses* (1988), *The Moor's Last Sigh* (1995), and *Shalimar the Clown* (2005). His signature style, adopting the manner and rhetorical gestures of fable and folding fantastical stories into the interstices of history, finds one of its smoothest and best realisations in this short story. His narration takes as its root the actual theft in 1963 of a relic, believed by many Muslims to be a hair of the prophet Muhammad, from the Hazratbal Mosque in Kashmir. Kashmir's fabled lakes and landscape are the setting for this exuberant tale of a hair which, like the writerly imagination, possesses all the force of a hurricane.

losing their balance, and asking in low, grave tones where he might go to engage the services of a dependably professional burglar. The young man's name was Atta, and the rogues in that part of town directed him gleefully into ever darker and less public alleys, until in a yard wet with the blood of a slaughtered chicken he was set upon by two men whose faces he never saw, robbed of the substantial bank-roll which he had insanely brought on his solitary excursion, and beaten within an inch of his life.

Night fell. His body was carried by anonymous hands to the edge of the lake, whence it was transported by shikara across the water and deposited, torn and bleeding, on the deserted embankment of the canal which led to the gardens of Shalimar. At dawn the next morning a flower-vendor was rowing his boat through water to which the cold of the night had given the cloudy consistency of wild honey when he saw the prone form of young Atta, who was just beginning to stir and moan, and on whose now deathly pale skin the sheen of wealth could still be made out dimly beneath an actual layer of frost.

The flower-vendor moored his craft and by stooping over the mouth of the injured man was able to learn the poor fellow's address, which was mumbled through lips that could scarcely move; whereupon, hoping for a large tip, the hawker rowed Atta home to a large house on the shores of the lake, where a beautiful but inexplicably bruised young woman and her distraught, but equally handsome mother, neither of whom, it was clear from their eyes, had slept a wink from worrying, screamed at the sight of their

Atta—who was the elder brother of the beautiful young woman—lying motionless amidst the funereally stunted winter blooms of the hopeful florist.

The flower-vendor was indeed paid off handsomely, not least to ensure his silence, and plays no further part in our story. Atta himself, suffering terribly from exposure as well as a broken skull, entered a coma which caused the city's finest doctors to shrug helplessly. It was therefore all the more remarkable that on the very next evening the most wretched and disreputable part of the city received a second unexpected visitor. This was Huma, the sister of the unfortunate young man, and her question was the same as her brother's, and asked in the same low, grave tones:

"Where may I hire a thief?"

The story of the rich idiot who had come looking for a burglar was already common knowledge in those insalubrious gullies, but this time the young woman added: "I should say that I am carrying no money, nor am I wearing any jewelry items. My father has disowned me and will pay no ransom if I am kidnapped; and a letter has been lodged with the Deputy Commissioner of Police, my uncle, to be opened in the event of my not being safe at home by morning. In that letter he will find full details of my journey here, and he will move Heaven and Earth to punish my assailants."

Her exceptional beauty, which was visible even through the enormous welts and bruises disfiguring her arms and forehead, coupled with the oddity of her inquiries, had attracted a sizable group of curious onlookers, and because her little speech seemed to them to cover just about everything, no one attempted to injure her in any way, although there were some raucous comments to the effect that it was pretty peculiar for someone who was trying to hire a crook to invoke the protection of a high-up policeman uncle.

She was directed into ever darker and less public alleys until finally in a gully as dark as ink an old woman with eyes which stared so piercingly that Huma instantly understood she was blind motioned her through a doorway from which darkness seemed to be pouring like smoke. Clenching her fists, angrily ordering her heart to behave normally, Huma followed the old woman into the gloom-wrapped house.

The faintest conceivable rivulet of candlelight trickled through the darkness; following this unreliable yellow thread (because she could no longer see the old lady), Huma received a sudden sharp blow to the shins and cried out involuntarily, after which she at once bit her lip, angry at having revealed her mounting terror to whoever or whatever waited before her, shrouded in blackness.

She had, in fact, collided with a low table on which a single candle burned and beyond which a mountainous figure could be made out, sitting cross-legged on the floor. "Sit, sit," said a man's calm, deep voice, and her legs, needing no more flowery invitation, buckled beneath her at the terse command. Clutching her left hand in her right, she forced her voice to respond evenly: "And you, sir, will be the thief I have been requesting?"

Shifting its weight very slightly, the shadow-mountain informed Huma that all criminal activity originating in this zone was well organised and also centrally controlled, so that all requests for what might be termed freelance work had to be channelled through this room.

He demanded comprehensive details of the crime to be committed, including a precise inventory of items to be acquired, also a clear statement of all financial inducements being offered with no gratuities excluded, plus, for filing purposes only, a summary of the motives for the application.

At this, Huma, as though remembering something, stiffened both in body and resolve and replied loudly that her motives were entirely a matter for herself; that she would discuss details with no one but the thief himself; but that the rewards she proposed could only be described as "lavish."

"All I am willing to disclose to you, sir, since it appears that I am on the premises of some sort of employment agency, is that in return for such lavish rewards I must have the most desperate criminal at your disposal, a man for whom life holds no terrors, not even the fear of God. The worst of fellows, I tell you—nothing less will do!"

At this a paraffin storm-lantern was lighted, and Huma saw facing her a grey-haired giant down whose left cheek ran the most sinister of scars, a cicatrice in the shape of the letter *Sín* in the Nastaliq script. She was gripped by the insupportably nostalgic notion that the bogeyman of her childhood nursery had risen up to confront her, because her ayah had always forestalled any incipient acts of disobedience by threatening Huma and Atta: "You don't watch out and I'll send that one to steal you away—that Sheikh Sín, the 'Thief of Thieves!"

Here, grey-haired but unquestionably scarred, was the notorious criminal himself—and was she out of her mind, were her ears playing tricks, or had he truly just announced that, given the stated circumstances, he himself was the only man for the job?

Struggling hard against the newborn goblins of nostalgia, Huma warned the fearsome volunteer that only a matter of extreme urgency and peril would have brought her unescorted into these ferocious streets.

"Because we can afford no last-minute backings-out," she continued, "I am determined to tell you everything, keeping back no secrets whatsoever. If, after hearing me out, you are still prepared to proceed, then we shall do everything in our power to assist you, and to make you rich."

The old thief shrugged, nodded, spat. Huma began her story.

Six days ago, everything in the household of her father, the wealthy moneylender Hashim, had been as it always was. At breakfast her mother had spooned khichri lovingly on to the moneylender's plate; the conversation had been filled with those expressions of courtesy and solicitude on which the family prided itself.

Hashim was fond of pointing out that while he was not a godly man he set great store by "living honourably

in the world." In that spacious lakeside residence, all out-
siders were greeted with the same formality and respect,
even those unfortunates who came to negotiate for small
fragments of Hashim's large fortune, and of whom he
naturally asked an interest rate of over seventy percent,
partly, as he told his khichri spooning wife, "to teach
these people the value of money; let them only learn that,
and they will be cured of this fever of borrowing borrowing all the time—so you see that if my plans succeed, I
shall put myself out of business!"

In their children, Atta and Huma, the moneylender
and his wife had successfully sought to inculcate the virtues of thrift, plain dealing, and a healthy independence
of spirit. On this, too, Hashim was fond of congratulating
himself.

Breakfast ended; the family members wished one another
a fulfilling day. Within a few hours, however, the glassy
contentment of that household, of that life of porcelain
delicacy and alabaster sensibilities, was to be shattered
beyond all hope of repair.

The moneylender summoned his personal shikara and
was on the point of stepping into it when, attracted by a
glint of silver, he noticed a small vial floating between the
boat and his private quay. On an impulse, he scooped it
out of the glutinous water.

It was a cylinder of tinted glass cased in exquisitely
wrought silver, and Hashim saw within its walls a silver
pendant bearing a single strand of human hair.

Closing his fist around this unique discovery, he muttered to the boatman that he'd changed his plans, and hurried to his sanctum, where, behind closed doors, he feasted his eyes on his find.

There can be no doubt that Hashim the moneylender knew from the first that he was in possession of the famous relic of the Prophet Muhammad, that revered hair whose theft from its shrine at Hazratbal mosque the previous morning had created an unprecedented hue and cry in the valley.

The thieves—no doubt alarmed by the pandemonium, by the procession through the streets of endless ululating crocodiles of lamentation, by the riots, the political ramifications, and by the massive police search which was commanded and carried out by men whose entire careers now hung upon the finding of this lost hair—had evidently panicked and hurled the vial into the gelatine bosom of the lake.

Having found it by a stroke of great good fortune, Hashim's duty as a citizen was clear: the hair must be restored to its shrine, and the state to equanimity and peace.

But the moneylender had a different notion.

All around him in his study was the evidence of his collector's mania. There were enormous glass cases full of impaled butterflies from Gulmarg, three dozen scale models in various metals of the legendary cannon Zamzama, innumerable swords, a Naga spear, ninety-four terracotta camels of the sort sold on railway station platforms, many samovars, and a whole zoology of tiny sandalwood animals, which had originally been carved to serve as children's bathtime toys.

"And after all," Hashim told himself, "the Prophet would have disapproved mightily of this relic-worship. He abhorred the idea of being deified! So, by keeping this hair from its distracted devotees, I perform—do I not?— a finer service than I would by returning it! Naturally, I don't want it for its religious value . . . I'm a man of the world, of this world. I see it purely as a secular object of great rarity and blinding beauty. In short, it's the silver vial I desire, more than the hair.

"They say there are American millionaires who purchase stolen art masterpieces and hide them away—they would know how I feel. I must, must have it!"

Every collector must share his treasures with one other human being, and Hashim summoned—and told—his only son Atta, who was deeply perturbed but, having been sworn to secrecy, only spilled the beans when the troubles became too terrible to bear.

The youth excused himself and left his father alone in the crowded solitude of his collections. Hashim was sitting erect in a hard, straight-backed chair, gazing intently at the beautiful vial.

It was well known that the moneylender never ate lunch, so it was not until evening that a servant entered the sanctum to summon his master to the dining table. He found Hashim as Atta had left him. The same, and not the same—for now the moneylender looked swollen, distended. His eyes bulged even more than they always had, they were red-rimmed, and his knuckles were white.

He seemed to be on the point of bursting! As though, under the influence of the misappropriated relic, he had filled up with some spectral fluid which might at any moment ooze uncontrollably from his every bodily opening.

He had to be helped to the table, and then the explosion did indeed take place.

Seemingly careless of the effect of his words on the carefully constructed and fragile constitution of the family's life, Hashim began to gush, to spume long streams of awful truths. In horrified silence, his children heard their father turn upon his wife, and reveal to her that for many years their marriage had been the worst of his afflictions. "An end to politeness!" he thundered. "An end to hypocrisy!"

Next, and in the same spirit, he revealed to his family the existence of a mistress; he informed them also of his regular visits to paid women. He told his wife that, far from being the principal beneficiary of his will, she would receive no more than the eighth portion which was her due under Islamic law. Then he turned upon his children, screaming at Atta for his lack of academic ability—"A dope! I have been cursed with a dope!"—and accusing his daughter of lasciviousness, because she went around the city barefaced, which was unseemly for any good Muslim girl to do. She should, he commanded, enter purdah forthwith.

Hashim left the table without having eaten and fell into the deep sleep of a man who has got many things off his chest, leaving his children stunned, in tears, and the dinner going cold on the sideboard under the gaze of an anticipatory bearer.

At five o'clock the next morning the moneylender forced his family to rise, wash, and say their prayers. From then on, he began to pray five times daily for the first time in his life, and his wife and children were obliged to do likewise.

Before breakfast, Huma saw the servants, under her father's direction, constructing a great heap of books in the garden and setting fire to it. The only volume left untouched was the Qur'an, which Hashim wrapped in a silken cloth and placed on a table in the hall. He ordered each member of his family to read passages from this book for at least two hours per day. Visits to the cinema were forbidden. And if Atta invited male friends to the house, Huma was to retire to her room.

By now, the family had entered a state of shock and dismay; but there was worse to come.

That afternoon, a trembling debtor arrived at the house to confess his inability to pay the latest installment of interest owed, and made the mistake of reminding Hashim, in somewhat blustering fashion, of the Qur'an's strictures against usury. The moneylender flew into a rage and attacked the fellow with one of his large collection of bullwhips.

By mischance, later the same day a second defaulter came to plead for time, and was seen fleeing Hashim's study with a great gash in his arm, because Huma's father had called him a thief of other men's money and had tried to cut off the wretch's right hand with one of the thirty-eight kukri knives hanging on the study walls.

These breaches of the family's unwritten laws of decorum alarmed Atta and Huma, and when, that evening, their mother attempted to calm Hashim down, he struck her on the face with an open hand. Atta leapt to his mother's defence and he, too, was sent flying.

"From now on," Hashim bellowed, "there's going to be some discipline around here!"

The moneylender's wife began a fit of hysterics which continued throughout that night and the following day, and which so provoked her husband that he threatened her with divorce, at which she fled to her room, locked the door and subsided into a raga of sniffling. Huma now lost her composure, challenged her father openly, and announced (with that same independence of spirit which he had encouraged in her) that she would wear no cloth over her face; apart from anything else, it was bad for the eyes.

On hearing this, her father disowned her on the spot and gave her one week in which to pack her bags and go.

By the fourth day, the fear in the air of the house had become so thick that it was difficult to walk around. Atta told his shock-numbed sister: "We are descending to gutter-level—but I know what must be done."

That afternoon, Hashim left home accompanied by two hired thugs to extract the unpaid dues from his two insolvent clients. Atta went immediately to his father's study. Being the son and heir, he possessed his own key to the moneylender's safe. This he now used, and removing the little vial from its hiding-place, he slipped it into his trouser pocket and re-locked the safe door.

Now he told Huma the secret of what his father had fished out of Lake Dal, and exclaimed: "Maybe I'm crazy—maybe the awful things that are happening have made me cracked—but I am convinced there will be no peace in our house until this hair is out of it."

His sister at once agreed that the hair must be returned, and Atta set off in a hired shikara to Hazratbal mosque. Only when the boat had delivered him into the throng of the distraught faithful which was swirling around the desecrated shrine did Atta discover that the relic was no longer in his pocket. There was only a hole, which his mother, usually so attentive to household matters, must have overlooked under the stress of recent events.

Atta's initial surge of chagrin was quickly replaced by a feeling of profound relief.

"Suppose," he imagined, "that I had already announced to the mullahs that the hair was on my person! They would never have believed me now—and this mob would have lynched me! At any rate, it has gone, and that's a load off my mind." Feeling more contented than he had for days, the young man returned home.

Here he found his sister bruised and weeping in the hall; upstairs, in her bedroom, his mother wailed like a brand-new widow. He begged Huma to tell him what had happened, and when she replied that their father, returning from his brutal business trip, had once again noticed a glint of silver between boat and quay, had once again scooped up the errant relic, and was consequently in a rage to end all rages, having beaten the truth out of her— then Atta buried his face in his hands and sobbed out his opinion, which was that the hair was persecuting them, and had come back to finish the job.

It was Huma's turn to think of a way out of their troubles.

While her arms turned black and blue and great stains spread across her forehead, she hugged her brother and whispered to him that she was determined to get rid of the hair at all costs—she repeated this last phrase several times.

"The hair," she then declared, "was stolen from the mosque; so it can be stolen from this house. But it must be a genuine robbery, carried out by a bona fide thief, not by one of us who are under the hair's thrall—by a thief so desperate that he fears neither capture nor curses."

Unfortunately, she added, the theft would be ten times harder to pull off now that their father, knowing that there had already been one attempt on the relic, was certainly on his guard.

"Can you do it?"

Huma, in a room lit by candle and storm-lantern, ended her account with one further question: "What assurances can you give that the job holds no terrors for you still?"

The criminal, spitting, stated that he was not in the habit of providing references, as a cook might, or a gardener, but he was not alarmed so easily, certainly not by any children's *djinni* of a curse. Huma had to be content with this boast, and proceeded to describe the details of the proposed burglary.

"Since my brother's failure to return the hair to the mosque, my father has taken to sleeping with his precious treasure under his pillow. However, he sleeps alone, and very energetically; only enter his room without waking him, and he will certainly have tossed and turned quite enough to make the theft a simple matter. When you have the vial, come to my room," and here she handed Sheikh Sín a plan of her home, "and I will hand over all the jewelry owned by my mother and myself. You will find . . . it is worth . . . that is, you will be able to get a fortune for it . . ." It was evident that her self-control was weakening and that she was on the point of physical collapse. "Tonight," she burst out finally. "You must come tonight!"

No sooner had she left the room than the old criminal's body was convulsed by a fit of coughing: he spat blood into an old vanaspati can. The great Sheikh, the "Thief of Thieves," had become a sick man, and every day the time drew nearer when some young pretender to his power would stick a dagger in his stomach. A lifelong addiction to gambling had left him almost as poor as he had been when, decades ago, he had started out in this line of work as a mere pickpocket's apprentice; so in the extraordinary commission he had accepted from the moneylender's daughter he saw his opportunity of amassing enough wealth at a stroke to leave the valley forever, and acquire the luxury of a respectable death which would leave his stomach intact.

As for the Prophet's hair, well, neither he nor his blind wife had ever had much to say for prophets—that was one thing they had in common with the moneylender's thunderstruck clan.

It would not do, however, to reveal the nature of this, his last crime, to his four sons. To his consternation, they had all grown up to be hopelessly devout men, who even spoke of making the pilgrimage to Mecca some day. "Absurd!" their father would laugh at them. "Just tell me how you will go?" For, with a parent's absolutist love, he had made sure they were all provided with a lifelong source of high income by crippling them at birth, so that, as they dragged themselves around the city, they earned excellent money in the begging business.

The children, then, could look after themselves.

He and his wife would be off soon with the jewel boxes of the moneylender's women. It was a timely chance indeed that had brought the beautiful bruised girl into his corner of the town.

That night, the large house on the shore of the lake lay blindly waiting, with silence lapping at its walls. A burglar's night: clouds in the sky and mists on the winter water. Hashim the moneylender was asleep, the only member of his family to whom sleep had come that night. In another room, his son Atta lay deep in the coils of his coma with a blood clot forming on his brain, watched over by a mother who had let down her long greying hair to show her grief, a mother who placed warm compresses on his head with gestures redolent of impotence. In a third bedroom Huma waited, fully dressed, amidst the jewel-heavy caskets of her desperation.

At last a bulbul sang softly from the garden below her window and, creeping downstairs, she opened a door to the bird, on whose face there was a scar in the shape of the Nastaliq letter Sín.

Noiselessly, the bird flew up the stairs behind her. At the head of the staircase they parted, moving in opposite directions along the corridor of their conspiracy without a glance at one another.

Entering the moneylender's room with professional ease, the burglar, Sín, discovered that Huma's predictions had been wholly accurate. Hashim lay sprawled diagonally across his bed, the pillow untenanted by his head, the prize easily accessible. Step by padded step, Sín moved towards the goal.

It was at this point that, in the bedroom next door, young Atta sat bolt upright in his bed, giving his mother a great fright, and without any warning—prompted by goodness knows what pressure of the blood clot upon his brain—began screaming at the top of his voice:

"*Thief! Thief! Thief!*"

It seems probable that his poor mind had been dwelling, in these last moments, upon his own father; but it is impossible to be certain, because having uttered these three emphatic words the young man fell back upon his pillow and died.

At once his mother set up a screeching and a wailing

and a keening and a howling so earsplittingly intense that they completed the work which Atta's cry had begun— that is, her laments penetrated the walls of her husband's bedroom and brought Hashim wide awake.

Sheikh Sín was just deciding whether to dive beneath the bed or brain the moneylender good and proper when Hashim grabbed the tiger-striped swordstick which always stood propped up in a corner beside his bed, and rushed from the room without so much as noticing the burglar who stood on the opposite side of the bed in the darkness. Sín stooped quickly and removed the vial containing the Prophet's hair from its hiding-place.

Meanwhile Hashim had erupted into the corridor, having unsheathed the sword inside his cane. In his right hand he held the weapon and was waving it about dementedly. His left hand was shaking the stick. A shadow came rushing towards him through the midnight darkness of the passageway and, in his somnolent anger, the moneylender thrust his sword fatally through its heart. Turning up the light, he found that he had murdered his daughter, and under the dire influence of this accident he was so overwhelmed by remorse that he turned the sword upon himself, fell upon it and so extinguished his life. His wife, the sole surviving member of the family, was driven mad by the general carnage and had to be committed to an asylum for the insane by her brother, the city's Deputy Commissioner of Police.

Sheikh Sín had quickly understood that the plan had gone awry.

Abandoning the dream of the jewel boxes when he was but a few yards from its fulfillment, he climbed out of Hashim's window and made his escape during the appalling events described above. Reaching home before dawn, he woke his wife and confessed his failure. It would be necessary, he whispered, for him to vanish for a while. Her blind eyes never opened until he had gone.

The noise in the Hashim household had roused their servants and even managed to awaken the nightwatchman, who had been fast asleep as usual on his charpoy by the street-gate. They alerted the police, and the Deputy Commissioner himself was informed. When he heard of Huma's death, the mournful officer opened and read the sealed letter which his niece had given him, and instantly led a large detachment of armed men into the light-repellent gullies of the most wretched and disreputable part of the city.

The tongue of a malicious cat burglar named Huma's fellow-conspirator; the finger of an ambitious bank robber pointed at the house in which he lay concealed; and although Sín managed to crawl through a hatch in the attic and attempt a rooftop escape, a bullet from the Deputy Commissioner's own rifle penetrated his stomach and brought him crashing messily to the ground at the feet of Huma's enraged uncle.

From the dead thief's pocket rolled a vial of tinted glass, cased in filigree silver.

The recovery of the Prophet's hair was announced at once on All-India Radio. One month later, the valley's

holiest men assembled at the Hazratbal mosque and formally authenticated the relic. It sits to this day in a closely
guarded vault by the shores of the loveliest of lakes in the
heart of the valley which was once closer than any other
place on earth to Paradise.

But before our story can properly be concluded, it is necessary to record that when the four sons of the dead Sheikh
awoke on the morning of his death, having unwittingly
spent a few minutes under the same roof as the famous
hair, they found that a miracle had occurred, that they
were all sound of limb and strong of wind, as whole as
they might have been if their father had not thought to
smash their legs in the first hours of their lives. They were,
all four of them, very properly furious, because the miracle had reduced their earning powers by 75 per cent, at
the most conservative estimate; so they were ruined men.

Only the Sheikh's widow had some reason for feeling
grateful, because although her husband was dead she had
regained her sight, so that it was possible for her to spend
her last days gazing once more upon the beauties of the
valley of Kashmir.

The Sound of Falling Leaves

Qurratulain Hyder

This morning I was standing at my backdoor, haggling with the vegetable-seller over the price of cabbage. The servant had already left for the market to get groceries. In the bathroom upstairs Viqar Sahib was studying his countenance in the full mirror, and humming as he shaved.

The doyenne of Urdu letters for most of the second half of the twentieth century, QURRATULAIN HYDER (1927–2007) wrote an eclectic and cosmopolitan fiction that ably gathers up the dynamics of a houschold and the long sweep of history in the same narrative space. One of her idiosyncrasies was translating her own work into English, often in such a way as to end up with not a version of that work, but a new work altogether (her great novel *Aag Ka Darya*, or *River of Fire*, is self-translated in this way). The questing, emotionally unsatisfied female protagonist of this story is typical of Hyder's work. But behind her we also see a many-hued Delhi that belonged to "the colourful, interesting world of unpartitioned India" and was part of the same civilizational continuum as the city of Lahore, which becomes a part of Pakistan in the "now" of the story, where the narrator finishes up.

As I argued with the vendor, I was also pondering over what to prepare for the evening meal. It was then that a car came to a stop in front of me. A woman peeped out, opened the door, and alighted. I was counting the change, which is why I didn't really notice her. She'd advanced a step before I raised my head and took a look.

"What . . . it's you!" she stammered, as though dumbstruck, and jerkily stopped in her tracks. It was as though she'd long thought me dead and was now confronted by my ghost.

The memory of the look of terror I saw in her eyes maddened me; I am obsessed with it, it's driving me up the wall.

This woman (even her name escapes me and I was too embarrassed to ask—she'd have taken it very badly) had studied with me at Queen Mary's in Delhi. This was some twenty years ago. I must have been about seventeen, but looked older because of my figure. My beauty had already begun to cause quite a stir. It was common practice in Delhi for mothers of eligible sons to go around from school to school appraising prospective brides. Afterwards a proposal would be sent to the home of any girl who won their approval. I found out that this girl's mother and aunts had taken a liking to me (having looked me over on the occasion of School Day) and were bent upon making me their daughter-in-law. These people lived on Nur Jahan Road, and the boy had recently got a job as an employee in the Reserve Bank of India, earning 150–200 rupees per month. Word was sent to my parents who lived in Meerut. But my mother was nursing grand dreams for me. Consequently, the offer was promptly declined.

Thereafter this girl remained my classmate for a while. Then she got married and left college. Today, after all these years, I saw her in a lane behind Mall Road in Lahore!

"Come on up, we can chat more comfortably over a cup of tea," I said to her politely.

"I'm in a hurry—just happened to pass by looking for the house of a family friend. I'll come again, some other time!"

Then, standing right there, she quickly recited the news of all our old friends and acquaintances, one by one—who's where and doing what: Salima is the wife of a brigadier—four kids; Farkhunda's husband is in the Foreign Service, her eldest daughter is studying in London; Raihana is the principal of such-and-such college; Sadia's brought back stacks of degrees from America and holds some high-powered job in Karachi. She was well up even on our Hindu classmates: Prabha's husband is a commodore in the Indian Navy, she lives in Bombay; Sarla is a station director of All India Radio; Lotika has become a famous artist. And so on and so forth. She was telling me all this, but I couldn't forget that look of horror in her eyes.

She said, "Whenever I get together with Sadia or Raihana in Karachi, we speak of you."

"Really?" I laughed hollowly—I could well imagine in what terms they spoke of me, the bitches. God! Had these people really been my friends? This two-faced tattler didn't even ask me what I was doing here, on the broken steps of this ratty tenement building, in a half-dark alley. She already knew.

Women's Intelligence Service is more efficient than Interpol. And anyway, my story is no secret. I have no social status, my existence is forgotten; I'm anonymous. That's why nobody cares about me—I don't even care about myself.

My name is Tanvir Fatima. My father was from Meerut, an average zamindar. Purdah was strictly observed in our house. I was even secluded from male cousins. I was a well-loved and indulged child. Having won many prizes in school I was admitted to Queen Mary's in Delhi for my matriculation.

I was sent to Aligarh for my college education. Aligarh Girl's College was the best period of my life. What a dreamy, rosy time! I'm not a sentimental person, but even now when I remember the college campus, its gardens, raindrops pattering on the leaves of trees, the cramped rooms and narrow verandahs of the hostel, my heart sinks in melancholy.

Then I came back to Delhi to do my MS. Raihana, Sadia, Prabha, and so on became my classmates. I never liked girls. I never liked people in general. Most of them were a mere waste of time.

I was arrogant because of my looks. And I, people said, was one in a million—my complexion the colour of gleaming glass, red-gold hair, an incredible figure. If I would don a Banarsi brocade sari, I would look like some maharani.

This was during the war. Or maybe the war had just ended that year—I don't remember exactly. Anyway, Delhi was like a garden in riotous bloom—daughters of millionaire businessmen and high-ranking government officials—Hindu, Sikh, Muslim would zoom about in gleaming limousines, making the rounds of social events: today a play at Miranda House, tomorrow a concert at Lady Irwin, Lady Hardinge or St. Stephen's, parties at Chelmsford Club, Roshanara, Imperial Gymkhana. Droves of army officers and bachelor civilians could be seen moving about everywhere it was quite a scene.

One day I went with Prabha and Sarla to visit Daljit Kaur. She was the daughter of a Sikh army contractor. We'd been invited to her garden party at a fancy mansion on King Edward Road. It was here that I met Major Khushvaqt Singh. He was a Chauhan Rajput from somewhere around Jhansi. Tall and raven-black, handlebar moustache, sparkling, beautiful teeth: he looked gorgeous when he laughed. He was a devotee of Ghalib, and punctuated every remark with a verse. He laughed heartily, talked, and spoke with impeccable manners. He invited us to accompany him to the cinema on another day. Sarla and Prabha did not go out with boys. Khushvaqt Singh was a friend of Daljit's brother. As I was trying to decide how to reply to him, Sarla whispered, "Say no. He's a big skirt-chaser." So I clammed up.

Those days, in New Delhi, the stories of one or two girls who had "gone bad" were circulating widely. I used to speculate fearfully about how girls from good families could hoodwink their parents and flirt around, making a spectacle of themselves. In the hostel we used to speculate about them. They seemed strange and mysterious despite the fact that they were just like us in appearance: well dressed, graceful, educated. . . .

"It's all false malicious rumour-mongering, ji," Sadia

would say, struggling to comprehend. "How could such reports really be true?"

"Actually, our society just hasn't been able to digest the notion of modern educated girls," Sarla would reply.

"The fact of the matter is that some girls lose their sense of balance," Raihana would opine.

In any case, we never could figure out how a few girls like us, among us, could conduct themselves in such a frightful fashion.

The next evening I was on my way to the laboratory when a sleek crimson-coloured car pulled up slowly to a stop near the Nicholson Memorial. Out of it jumped Khushvaqt Singh, his beautiful teeth flashing in the dark.

"Don't tell me you forgot our appointment, young lady."

"I beg your pardon?" I asked in confusion.

"Come along, one must not slog away in the laboratory after sundown."

Quite involuntarily I looked around, got into the car, and slouched down. We went to Connaught Place and saw an English film.

The next day too.

I moved about with him for a week in this fashion. He lodged at Maiden's. By the end of that week I had become Major Khushvaqt Singh's mistress.

I am not literary, I haven't studied Chinese, Japanese, Russian, English, or even Urdu poetry. To my mind, reading literature is a waste of time. From the age of fifteen science has been my life, waking or sleeping. I have no idea about metaphysical concepts, or the mystical experience. I had no time for poetry or philosophy either then or now. Nor do I command a vocabulary of large, ambiguous, arcane terms.

Anyway, within fifteen days just about everyone in the college knew about me. Well, I had always been profoundly self-reliant and couldn't have cared less. Earlier too I didn't socialize much. Sarla and her crowd now looked at me as though I'd landed from planet Mars, or had horns sprouting from my head. After I left the dining hall they'd discuss my case for hours. Through their Intelligence Service they were kept apprised of how Khushvaqt and I spent every moment—where we'd gone that evening, which ballroom in Delhi we'd gone dancing at (Khushvaqt was a fantastic dancer and he taught me how to dance too), in which shops Khushvaqt had bought me what gifts, and so on.

Khushvaqt Singh used to beat me a lot. And loved me too, as no other man on earth could have loved a woman.

Several months passed. My MS previous exams were about to begin. I became immersed again in my studies. After the exams were over he said, "My Life! Sweetheart! Let's slip away to some quiet hillstation—Solan, Dalhousie, Lansdowne." I went to Meerut for a few days and then returned to Delhi telling my father (my mother had died while I was in my third year) that I had to study hard for my final year. There was too much chance of running into someone we know at North Indian hillstations, so we went down south, to Ooty. We stayed there a full month. When Khushvaqt's holidays were over, we returned to Delhi and put up in a bungalow in Timarpur.

A week before term commenced, Khushvaqt and I had a huge fight. He thrashed me well and proper. He hit me so much that my face was covered with blood, and my arms and legs were black and blue. The cause of the fight was that wretched Christian fiancée of his, who oozed in from God knows where and was spewing venom against me all over town. If she'd had her way she'd have chewed me up and spat me out. This treacherous woman had been in the army during the war and met Khushvaqt in the Burma campaign. Who knows how Khushvaqt ended up promising to marry her. But after meeting me he was determined to return her the engagement ring.

That night in that lonely bungalow in Timarpur he came crying to me with hands clasped and begged me to marry him, saying he'd die otherwise. I told him never, no way, not until doomsday. I, a very high-born Syed, marry a black blob of tobacco, a Hindu Jat, and disgrace my family? No, never! I was dreaming that a handsome scion of noble Muslim lineage would appear sooner or later leading a wedding procession to marry me. The traditional Quran and mirror-ceremony would be performed and with all the ceremonial dress and drama of a Muslim wedding, I would leave my own home and go to his. My sisters-in-law would block the door, haranguing until the "demand money" had been extorted from their brother. Dancing women would come with their drums to sing the traditional wedding songs. And so on and so forth.

And hadn't I seen the disastrous end that Hindu-Muslim marriages came to? A number of people, either from a desire to be progressive or in the throes of passionate feelings, had gone off and married Hindus, only to get separated within a year or less. Not to mention the uprooting and turmoil caused in the lives of the children, belonging neither here nor there. . . .

At my refusal, Khushvaqt kicked me and pulverized me with his feet and hit me with his shoes. And two days later he took off for Agra with that lousy female Katherine Dharamdas and married her in a civil ceremony.

When I arrived at the hostel at the beginning of the new term, my head and face were bandaged up. I wrote to my father that I'd been conducting an experiment in the laboratory with dangerous materials. There'd been an explosion and my face had got slightly burned, but I was perfectly fine now, and that he shouldn't worry.

The girls already knew and discreetly refrained from even formally enquiring about my health. After such a huge scandal, I should have been turned out of the hostel. However, the warden was a friend of Khushvaqt's, so everybody kept quiet. No one had any solid evidence, anyway. People are, as a matter of course, hell-bent on damaging the reputation of college girls.

I remember that time well, as though it were yesterday. It must have been ten or eleven in the morning. The girls were arriving from the railway station, driving through the gates in tongas. Baggage was being piled under the banyan, there was a tremendous furore. When I got off my tonga, and they saw my bandaged head, they were as bewildered as if they'd all been mesmerized by a snake. I had the chowkidar load my belongings and went up to my room. When I returned downstairs for lunch, those bitches spoke to me of this and that in such a manner as to make it clear that they knew the real nature of my accident, and weren't mentioning it in order to save me from embarrassment. One of them, who was the ring-leader and role model of this evil tribe, delivered a verdict at the dinner table to the effect that I was in terms of modern psychology, a nymphomaniac. (This pronounce-ment, transmitted through my own spies, was immedi-ately relayed up to my room, where I was busy studying by the table lamp near the window.) It was common, in such matters, she further opined, that one fish fouled up the entire pond. That was why some people said women's liberation was a dangerous thing, etc., etc.

As for me, I couldn't agree with them more. I myself wondered why a number of virtuous girls from good fam-ilies who had attained higher education should go astray. There was a theory to the effect that those girls whose IQ was low were the ones who strayed. Intelligent beings would never deliberately take a step that led toward perdi-tion; but I had also seen well-brought-up girls of sharp understanding go astray. Another theory attributed it to a leisurely, luxurious life, hunger for expensive presents, inclination to romance, desire for adventure, or simply boredom, or rebellion against the old bondage of purdah. It must be all these things, what other explanation could there be?

As soon as I was done with my first-term exams, Khushvaqt again presented himself. He phoned the labo-ratory to say that I should meet him at six o'clock at Niru-la's restaurant. I did just that. He had deposited Katherine at his parents' place and come to Delhi on army business. This time we flew to Bombay for a week.

After that we used to meet every second or third month. A year passed. This time when he came, he was on his way from Lucknow to Lahore and had a few hours' stopover at Palam airport. As soon as he arrived in Delhi he sent a close friend to fetch me in a car. This boy was the son of a Muslim tycoon of Delhi. Well, not quite a boy, even at that time he was around forty, married, a family man. He was dark and gangly like a palm tree, spoke bad English, and had the face of a fowler. And was uncouth.

After this Khushvaqt never returned. Because now I had become Faruq's mistress.

Faruq presented me as his "fiancée" to Delhi's high society. Muslims are entitled to four marriages after all, so this wasn't such a horrible thing to do. At least, not from the socio-religious point of view. Why shouldn't he want, despite the existence of an illiterate, purdah-donning wife of middle age, to marry an educated girl who could conduct herself properly in company? Then, too, in wealthy circles anything goes, whereas middle-class rules say, don't do this, don't do that. Now, during long vacations Faruq took me on trips to Calcutta, Lucknow, Ajmer—what places didn't I see with him? He showered me with diamonds. I wrote to my father that I was travelling with fellow university students. Or that I had been invited to participate in a science conference at such-and-such place. Despite all this, I still cared about maintaining a high academic record.

I fared badly in the final exam, and went home. Just then the Partition riots broke out. Faruq wrote to me in Meerut that I should go immediately to Pakistan and that he would meet me there. I had already decided to leave. My father, too, was extremely concerned and did not want me to remain in India with things as they were, where the honour of daughters of respectable Muslim families was in such perpetual jeopardy. Pakistan was our own Islamic homeland, after all. Safe and civilized. As for his own situation, father could not leave the country right away because of his property and lands. My two brothers were both very young, and after mother's death father had sent them to the Deccan, to our aunt in Hyderabad.

My results came out, breaking my heart—I got only a third division.

When the storm of riots had begun to abate a little I came by air to Lahore. Faruq came with me. His scheme was to open a branch of his company in Pakistan with the head office in Lahore. I would be the owner of the business. And we would get married there. He would not leave Delhi permanently for his father was a nationalist opposed to the creation of Pakistan. Our plan was for Faruq to visit me in Lahore from Delhi every two or three months. Lahore was in chaos. Although allotments of the best housing could be had in the best neighbourhoods, Faruq knew no one here. Still, he found a smallish house in Sant Nagar, took it in my name, and deposited me there. And to keep me company he had the family of a distant relative to come and stay with me. They had arrived in Lahore as refugees and were wandering about homeless.

I was in such consternation due to all this sudden change that I couldn't really understand what had happened. Where was that colourful, interesting world of unpartitioned India, and where this dark and dingy house in Lahore of 1948? Robbed of a homeland, great God! What heartrending times I've seen.

I became so disoriented that I didn't even look for employment. I was not worried about money because

Faruq had left ten thousand rupees in my name. Only ten thousand. He himself was a millionaire. But I was just not aware of the world around me at this particular time. (I'm still not.)

The days passed. I lay on my bed from morning till night. Faruq's distant aunt or great-aunt—whatever that old woman was—ate paan after paan as she recounted the misfortunes of her escape from India and the glories of her lost home. Or I would teach algebra to her daughter, who was doing her matric. Her son was running the apology of a business that Faruq had set up in Lahore.

Faruq would make a trip five or six times a year. Life in Lahore was gradually returning to normal. When he came, my days passed more brightly. His aunt would prepare Mughal delicacies for him. I would go to the hairdresser on Mall Road and have my hair set. In the evenings we would visit the Gymkhana Club. And there, at a corner table, over a glass of beer, Faruq would tell me all the goings-on in Delhi. He would speak tirelessly, then suddenly fall silent and stare at the faces of unknown people entering the room. He never once mentioned marriage, nor did I bring it up. I was now jaded and gone to seed. It was all the same to me. When he returned to Delhi I would write to him every fifteenth day about my own well-being and that of his business, and that when he came next he should bring such-and-such saris from this shop or that in Connaught Place or Chandni Chowk, because you couldn't get good saris in Pakistan.

One day a letter arrived from my uncle in Meerut that father had died. I was reminded of a line from a poem lamenting the Prophet's death: "When Ahmad whom God had sent, did not live forever, who would?" I have no truck with sentiment. But my father had loved me dearly and his death was a hard blow. Faruq wrote me heartfelt, tender letters and they afforded me some consolation. He wrote: "Keep saying your prayers. These are evil times. A black storm is moving through the world; the sun is hung low in the sky, as though doomsday were near. No telling what might happen from one moment to the next." Like most businessmen he was extremely pious and superstitious. He frequented the shrine of Ajmer, consulted astrologers, pandits, pirs, fakirs, heeded good or bad omens, and believed in every kind of soothsayer.

I tried saying my prayers five times a day. But every time I prostrated myself, I had this overwhelming urge to laugh.

There was a tremendous need in the country for women science teachers. When the administrators of a local college asked me, I began teaching, even though I absolutely hate teaching. After a while I was sent to a girl's college in a remote, backward district in Punjab. I worked there for several years. My girl students used to ask me, "Miss Tanvir, you are so sweet and pretty, why don't you marry that millionaire fiancé of yours?"

I really had no answer. This was a new country, new people, a new society. Here no one knew of my past, there could be a good man here prepared to marry me (not that I was that enamoured of handsome, straight gentlemen anyway—what was I to do?). Tales of Delhi remained in Delhi. And I had also seen how each and every "fast" woman had now become a paragon of virtue. Look at Edith Hariram and Rani Khan, for instance.

Now, Faruq too came less and less frequently. We used

to meet as people who had been married for years and years, for whom there was nothing new, nothing left to know, and it was time for peace, calm, and rest. Recently Faruq's daughter had got married in Delhi, his son had been to Oxford, his wife was a chronic asthmatic. Faruq had opened up branches of his business in various foreign countries; he was building a new bungalow in Naini Tal. . . . He would relate to me the entire familial goings-on and business matters while I kept him supplied with paan.

One time when I came to Lahore during college vacation Faruq introduced me to an old friend of his, Mr. Viqar Husain Khan. He was unique in his own way—ugly and slimy, of inky-black complexion, about forty-five years old. I had first seen him in Delhi, where he ran a dance school. The only son of a genteel family, he had run away from home while still a child and travelled from country to country with the circus, carnivals, and theatre companies—Singapore, Hong Kong, Shanghai, London. He'd made marriages with women of various ethnic and national origins. His present wife was a Marwari money-lender's daughter from Orissa. He had abducted her from Calcutta. I had seen her twelve or fifteen years before in Delhi. She was a shortish attractive woman. Her face wore a strange expression of sadness, but I had heard that she was a devoted wife. She would get fed up with her husband's ill treatment and go away, but a few days later she'd be back again. Khan Sahib had opened a school on the third floor of a building in Connaught Circus, where he taught ballroom dancing. His wife and two Anglo-Indian girls constituted the "staff." During the war the school was fabulously successful. Once I had gone there with Khushvaqt to one of their Sunday "jam sessions." I had heard that Viqar Sahib's wife was like an avatar of the virtuous Anasuya—at her husband's behest she would befriend various girls, extending sisterly affection to them—and bring them to meet him. And the dutiful girl did just as she was told. One time she even came to our hostel and urged several girls to come for tea with her at Barakhamba Road.

After Partition, Viqar Sahib made his way to Lahore devastated and penniless, as the saying goes. He got himself allotted a flat behind the Mall Road and set up his school. Business was slow at first. A pall had been cast over people's hearts. Who felt like dancing and singing? Before Partition this apartment had housed an Arya Samaj music school. The hall had a wooden floor. On the side were two small rooms, a bathroom and a kitchen, and in the front a wooden balcony and a rickety staircase. A board hung askew from the balcony lattice which read, "Hind Mata Sangeet Mahavidyalaya." He took it down and replaced it with "Viqar's School of Ballroom and Tap Dancing." He cut out colour pictures of Gene Kelley, Fred Astaire, Frank Sinatra, and Doris Day from American film magazines, pasted them on the dilapidated walls of the hall, and the school was ready. The Khan Sahib had brought a small collection of records with him from Delhi. Borrowing money from Faruq, he bought some second-hand furniture and a gramophone in Lahore. God bless the restless, adventure-seeking college boys and nouveau-riche ladies who wanted to become rapidly westernized! Within two or three years his efforts had been handsomely repaid.

Because of his friendship with Faruq, my relationship

with Viqar became something like one between an elder brother and a sister-in-law. He would look after me, and his wife would cook and sew with me hour after hour while talking of old times. Poor thing, she was as affectionate towards me as an older sister-in-law. They were a childless couple. It was an unhappy, colourless, and drab union. There are people like that in this world!

I got into a fight with the snooty, U.S.-returned principal of my college. If she said black, I said white. In my own way, I was no less than the finicky Tana Shah, the king who was known for his delicate temperament. I threw my resignation at the face of the College Committee and returned to Sant Nagar, Lahore. I was fed up with teaching. I could get a scholarship and go abroad and do my PhD. But I procrastinated on this plan, too. Some day I would go to the American Consulate, where they disbursed scholarships. Or some day I must go to the British Council. Or I ought to send in a scholarship application to the Ministry of Education.

More and more time elapsed. What would I do in some foreign place? What forts would I conquer? What target could I shoot at? I don't know what I was waiting for.

One day Viqar Sahib came to me, beside himself, and said, "Your sister-in-law has gone crazy again. She has gone back to India. And she's not coming back."

"How can that be?" I asked, rather carelessly, and put some water on to boil for tea.

"The fact is I divorced her. She'd become such a battle-axe." He sat down on the hard bed in front and, like a typical husband, began to narrate his wife's shortcomings. And then proceeded to try to convince me of his own complete innocence.

I listened to the whole story, unconcerned. Everything in life was just as unimportant, uninteresting, and meaningless as this.

Some days later he came to me and muttered: "The servants are harassing me. I don't suppose you could come over some time and set things straight at your brother's house? Scold the servants. How can I manage both school and home?" He whined in such a way as to imply that the affairs of his home were my responsibility.

Several days later I packed up my things and shifted to Viqar Sahib's rooms. And became his assistant dance instructor.

A full month later, last Sunday, Viqar Sahib called a maulvi, and with his two petty servants as witnesses, had the marriage solemnized.

Nowadays I'm completely absorbed in household chores. My youth and beauty are but the stuff of a past legend. I don't care at all for parties, excitement, and other such nonsense, although "cha-cha-cha" and "calypso" and the roar of "rock-'n'-roll" are ever present in the house. Well, it's home.

Right now I have offers from several colleges to teach chemistry. But where would I find the time, what with my housewifely duties? You hire a servant one day, the next day he's gone. I never wanted much. Just a medium-sized house, maybe, with a car so that I could get around without too much difficulty, and my peers wouldn't look down upon me. And, if a few people were to come to visit, I would have a proper place to seat them. That was all I wanted.

Nowadays we bring in fifteen hundred to two thousand a month, which is more than enough for the needs of just one man and his wife. If a person has enough to satisfy his or her requirements then all sorrows vanish.

Once she gets married a protective ceiling closes in on a woman. Who knows how the young women of today get along, how they slip through. No matter how much I think about it, it seems strange to me, and I just wonder.

It isn't as though I had been a flirt. Except for Khush-vaqt, Faruq, and this black-faced son of a giant who's my husband, I never knew any other man. Perhaps I wasn't such a bad person. I don't really know what I was or am. Raihana, Sadia, Prabha, and this girl whose eyes filled with terror when she saw me—maybe they know me better than I know myself.

What's the point in thinking about Khushvaqt? Those days are long gone. For all I know he's a brigadier or major-general by now, leading troops against the Chinese on the Assam border. Or seated in some mess in some nice lush cantonment in India, twirling his moustache and smiling. Maybe he's been killed long ago on the Kashmir front. Who knows?

On dark nights I lie awake quietly, my eyes open. Science has acquainted me with a number of secrets of the universe. I've read countless chemistry books, thought for hours and hours. But still I'm scared. I get really scared in the middle of the night.

Khushvaqt Singh, Khushvaqt Singh, why should you have anything to do with me now?

Translated from Urdu by Carla Petievich

The Accountant

Kunal Basu

BESIDES BEING A CLEVER MAN, *an architect must be a mathematician and an artist, a historian and an engineer. . . .* Mr. Ray looked up from his book and cleared his throat as if to read aloud to his wife, then turned his gaze back. . . . *He should be a good writer worthy of conveying his plans in minute detail, a skilled draftsman versed in geometry and optics, possess a good ear for music and show no ignorance of the motion of heavenly bodies . . .*

Sitting on the bed, Mrs. Beena Roy continued to fold

One of the most original of the current generation of Indian writers in English, KUNAL BASU (1956–) roves boldly across space and time in his work. His three novels—*The Opium Clerk*, *The Miniaturist*, and *Racists*—all employ some original and startling premise. This story, comic and poignant by turns, perhaps one of the best stories ever written about a monument, employs the trope of reincarnation to take us far back into Mughal India. We see the Taj Mahal not as the familiar and beloved monument as it is today, but as a dream still waiting to be realised, and our narrator is the agent.

---

dry laundry, which took up almost the entire evening after she returned from work at the income tax office—buttoning up shirts and matching the sleeves, pressing her palm down over the ugly bumps of a starched sari, folding napkins into bunny caps or slapping the pyjama bottoms to rid them of ungainly static. In the end, they lay in neat stacks before her, a chastened bunch, requiring no ironing. It was a routine as well as an excuse to withdraw from the pointless chitter-chatter of long married couples that added less than pepper and salt to plain evenings with television and occasional incursions by neighbours. She was used to living quietly without children after twenty childless years of marriage and without pets after a Maltese had triggered her husband's asthma.

Mr. Ray read silently, waiting for the nightly news to quicken the evening's pace—the flurry of dinner, washing up, making up the bed and selecting items from his wife's neat pile for the next working day. After twenty years in the same job there wasn't much to discuss about work, although he made a point of promptly disclosing any rise in salary so that his wife could duly report it on their joint income tax returns. Barring a tiff or two over visiting relatives, there was no hint of the type of "marital troubles" his peers routinely discussed, and he was proud to have a wife who didn't overspend or gossip with neighbours, embarrass him in public in any way, or burden him with sickly in-laws. She was as indifferent to his reading as he was to her folding. Even when they were younger, each had been mindful of the other's routines and shied away from upsetting the even pace of an easy life. The only oddity that he had noticed was his wife's refusal to spell her last name in the same way as he did—not Beena Ray, wife of Bimal Ray, but Beena *Roy*. She had avoided the "anglicised Ray" as the only mark of discord—the name-plate on their South Delhi flat puzzled the neighbours and prompted postmen to ask a few questions before a parcel for Ray could be delivered to Roy or that for Roy to Ray.

Mostly, he read for self-improvement—manuals and refreshers with the occasional "path-breaking study" thrown in, that his boss demanded every employee read, offering words of encouragement to the half-willing and threats to the rest. Mr. Ray, of course, needed neither threat nor encouragement, simply fodder for his evening routine in the company of his silent wife. It wasn't exactly true that he never shared his readings with Beena, but limited them to taxation matters that could help her improve as well. On these occasions he'd clear his throat and begin reading, as if his wife expected him to do so, often going over a paragraph twice for emphasis. Hands parted to take in the full breadth of a bedcover, she'd listen with her face hidden behind then offer her comment after folding the piece to perfection.

. . . *He must perform both manual and brain work for which he should be free of disease and disability.* . . . Mr. Ray laid down the heavy volume on the stool before him then started to read aloud. "An architect must be free of the seven sins; he must not have excessive desire for gain and be generous to the point of forgiving his rivals. . . ."

Mrs. Roy frowned, threading her fingers to bunch together the mosquito nettings—the most difficult of all items to fold properly—and cast a quick glance at the

TV to check if it was indeed her husband's voice she was hearing.

"Geography will tell him if the chosen land is suitable, astronomy guide him in setting the building to the right proportions, physics will inform him of the conduct of rivers and lakes that may surround his creation, theology advise him of its proper role among men. Besides being a jack-of-all-trades, an architect must be accurate." Mr. Ray shut the volume and wet his lips ready to conclude his reading, "Above all, he must be a devil for detail."

As she put away the neat stacks into the linen closet, Beena Roy glanced suspiciously at the volume on the stool, *A Guide for Architects in Medieval India*, and offered her own conclusion, "Just as an accountant like you."

He woke promptly at two, at the exact hour he had woken every night during the past month. Sitting up on the bed, he wondered if he should wake Beena up and tell her everything. His gaze slipped through the open window and crossed the boundary wall of their gated colony, into the deserted roads and sleepy shrines. Then on it soared over the national highway, flying straight as a crow through the dustbowl of Northern India. It skirted the Yamuna on its way down the plains and came to rest on a flat bed beaten out of the alluvial soil where the river changed course from south to east. Agra! Mr. Ray felt he had arrived, yet again, at the very spot he knew only too well. He sensed a familiar rush of excitement as he saw a much younger man who bore him a passing resemblance stride past throngs of labourers assembled on the flattened riverfront, struck with frenzy just as an event was about to unfold. Words rang in his ears. . . . *Mimar! Mimar!* that followed the young man.

Mimar . . . the architect. He could understand everything—greetings, complaints, even a sly request for a leave of absence—muttered in a dozen tongues, knowing instantly that he had arrived at the Taj, not one of the world's wonders as it is called today but the wonder that it was even as it was being built more than three hundred years ago by a team of clever architects. Mr. Ray felt certain that *he* was the Chota Mimar—the young architect arrived from Persia at the call of Hindustan's emperor. A shudder went through him as he closed his eyes and realized what he was thinking. Ever since these strange things had begun, starting always in his dreams and lingering on even when he was fully awake, he had had to pinch himself to see if indeed the recollections of his past life were as real as commonplace memory—the memory of his move to Delhi from Calcutta twenty years ago or that of his marriage to Beena. He was worried that he had contracted some kind of rare disease, perhaps of the brain, that was turning him mad. And he couldn't even begin to imagine what would happen if any of this were to become public knowledge. Who would believe him, the successful accountant with decades of uninterrupted service and a steadfast marriage now claiming to remember his past life—not just any life but as the Taj's architect—trust what he saw and felt every night, the flashes that inexplicably reminded him of who he once was? Rubbish! He himself would've thought so, nothing but hocus-pocus. Yet, he couldn't bring himself to deny the thrill, the secret pleasure of dipping into his memory that drew him to the edge of his bed every night as he woke to relive his dream.

It was the first urs of the queen's death, the day of union of her soul with the Eternal. Mr. Ray smiled sadly, knowing what was to follow. He, the Chota Mimar, had heard rumours in Agra—the body had already been dug up from the makeshift grave in the Deccan where Mumtaz had died. Her corpse was on its way, accompanied by her lady-in-waiting and the second eldest prince. She'd be given a second burial at the western garden of the riverfront terrace that afternoon and a small dome would be raised over it quickly to shield her from the eyes of a thousand labourers building her final resting place, the Taj Mahal.

He could even remember the precise date—1632, the first Wednesday of the month of Zil-Qa'da. All those assembled were sulking under the Agra sun—nobles who had arrived on their horses and elephants, pious men who had come armed with the Koran, scholars and traders along with the high and low of the empire gathered in tents fitted with fine carpets and awnings. The labourers had withdrawn to their quarters for the day—the masons and stonecutters, carvers, inlayers, and their masters—but the team of architects was still present led by Ustad Ahmad Lahori. *The Great Pretender!* Mr. Ray could hear himself snorting under his breath as he stood beside the Lahore architect who had managed to crawl his way into the Emperor's sight without even an ounce of talent, ushering in his cronies as well who couldn't tell a stable from a tomb, a rauza from a simple garden. Had it not been for the Emperor's father-in law, himself a Persian, there wouldn't be a place for the Chota Mimar in Agra. Didn't the queen's mausoleum deserve the very best? Its plans drawn not simply from Hindustan but from Isphafan and Constantinople, Kabul and Samarkand—from the whole world? And where else but in Persia would one find the best of the best?

Everyone, including him, understood the Emperor's grief. Catching a glimpse of the widower Shah Jahan sitting crestfallen beside his father-in-law, he had mistaken him for a fakir—eyes sunk into deep hollows, hair turned grey, counting a string of rosary. He recalled bazaar gossip—the Emperor has stopped listening to music, given up wine, shed jewellery. Unlike his ancestors, the loss of a wife has meant more to him than an absence of hawa-i-nafs—the games one enjoys with a perfumed body—an absence no embrace could ever fill. He could hear sniggering voices around him . . . *if he goes on like this, poor Mumtaz will be forced to give up the joys of paradise and return to earth . . . !*

He thought he had sneaked away from the assembly to share a laugh with his Persian friend, the artist Mir Sultan, and a puff or two from the opium pipe carefully hidden underneath his ceremonial gown. No . . . it couldn't be so, Mr. Ray corrected himself. His friend, the scoundrel, was still asleep, as he learnt later, hung over from the night before.

There was a commotion, he recalled, as Shah Jahan rose to distribute alms to a group of beggars assembled in the terrace. By the time the coffin arrived, many had fainted from the heat. Then the Emperor started to recite the Fatiha, the very first and the briefest verse of the

Koran . . . *In the name of God, the Lord of Mercy, the Giver of Mercy!*

As he took a gulp of water from the glass beside his bed, Mr. Ray sighed, wondering why he had recalled such a tragic scene in great detail. He felt sad, just as he had felt in his past life—the Chota Mimar's heart turned heavy at the sight of the poor husband cradling the coffin like his bride; the Emperor—the Shadow of God—reduced to a mere shadow of himself in grief.

Yet, in his early days in Agra, he, the young Persian architect, had felt nothing but contempt for the Mughals. Building a house on earth to resemble the queen's palace in paradise! He had taken Lahori's instructions with a grain of salt. Like the other garden tombs of the city it was to have a marble mausoleum flanked on either side by a mosque and a guest house, a Khorasani garden up to the great gateway along with a forecourt, quarters for the tomb attendants, a bazaar and a caravanserai. The youngest among the architects, he had broken into peals of laughter when shown the design of the mausoleum's dome.

"It looks like a guava!"

"Shh . . ." A fellow architect had covered his mouth, cautioned him against speaking his mind. The Emperor himself was the master architect, the real ones charged simply with drawing up his dictates on paper.

It was a hodgepodge, the Chota Mimar had concluded after careful scrutiny. The gate stolen from Constantinople, the garden from Kabul, the minarets from Arabia, even the dome was a vain imitation of Jerusalem's Rock. They were Mughals after all, he had thought—upstarts.

One needed to visit the tomb of their great ancestor Timur in Samarkand for proof—that obscene blue dome sticking up into the sky as if to rival heaven itself! What else could they do but steal from others? In the early months, he had had to console himself—it was just a matter of time before the Taj would be built and he'd make his way back to Persia. Turning over on his bed and listening to Beena snore, Mr. Ray wondered why his rich memory didn't offer a hint of his past life spent in his native land, why he remembered nothing about his Persian parents, his brothers and sisters. Not a trace remained of his journey to Hindustan, only the years he had spent in Agra, as if his life had started and ended there.

An Agra native, Mr. Mehta, his boss, knew and cared little about the Taj. "It cost half a million rupees to build and generated a yearly revenue of just twenty thousand from the mango trees!" —he quipped flippantly after Mr. Ray had delicately brought up the matter. The office peon was better equipped, entrusted with the duty of delivering sensitive documents once a year to their sole client in Agra, always ready with bus and train timetables at his fingertips for the 193-kilometre journey. Mr. Ray wasn't starved for facts, simply desirous to dwell on the subject every now and then in the same way as one dwells upon one's hometown or a place visited long ago. The very mention of a familiar name might, he hoped, help him keep silent about his past life, give him strength to resist the urge to reveal everything and make a fool of himself. Keeping his head down over annual reports and balance sheets, he could imagine the shock and the daily dose of

sniggering that'd inevitably follow should he succumb to
a moment of weakness.

He had started to leave the office early, secretly by the
back, an excuse ready on his lips. If asked he'd say he was
on his way to meet a client or to hand over a report to the
Auditor General's office. If his boss were to catch him,
he'd lie about Beena, confer some terrible disease upon
her. He was leaving to take his wife for a consultation,
he'd tell Mr. Mehta.

Following his instinct he went first to the local library
and then to the National Archives. It didn't take him
long to lose his shyness asking the librarian for books
he'd never had any reason to consult before. The more
he read about the Mughals—their gardens, tombs, for-
tresses and palaces—the more he sensed the architect
within himself. He'd grasp unknown facts with ease; nod
in agreement with passages no accountant could possibly
fathom, or argue with an invisible author who he knew
for a fact to have committed a careless error. Nothing, of
course, excited him more than examining the plans of the
Taj—its architectural drawings preserved under layers of
dust in the Archives.

Ah! The Hast Bihist! Sitting all by himself in the dark
reading hall, Mr. Ray could hardly contain himself. Hast
Bihist—the eight-chambered paradise that was to serve
as a model for the queen's mausoleum. He traced the lines
of the perfect square on the crumbling page lovingly with
his fingertip. Four simple lines divided the square into
nine parts, suggesting a domed chamber at the centre,
forehalls in the middle of the four sides, and Baghdadi
towers at each corner. From experience he knew it to be

typically Persian with Byzantine ancestry. Lit by the setting sun, the plan glowed in his hands. Mr. Ray felt he
was gazing not at a piece of paper but at the completed
mausoleum set amidst the gardens of Agra. Even so, his
face hardened as he recalled the fate of the plan drawn up
by the Taj's architects. What was the use of presenting
the Emperor with the Hast Bihist when his pen would
flow freely over it, cutting open a terrace here, inserting
an arch there, replacing towers with domes, just to please
a pair of mortal eyes? *Allah!* He bowed his head over the
desk.

"Tea . . . ?"

Mr. Ray jerked his head up, the spell about to be
broken by the voice of the Archive's assistant. He was a
young man, ordinary looking, a smile to cover his disappointment at holding such a lowly job, unlike most of his
friends. Must've fared poorly in his exams to deserve this,
Mr. Ray thought, wiping his glasses as he returned to his
office-beaten self. The two of them had struck up a rap-
port—the shy assistant taking the middle-aged visitor to
be a scholar working on his next book, or a hobbyist with
time to kill. On arrival, Mr. Ray would find the oversized
folios waiting for him neatly arranged on a desk by the
window. The assistant would bring over a moist sponge
to wet his fingers should the pages prove to be too dry to
turn, a pair of gloves if too brittle; he'd supply a magnify-
ing glass and offer tea when the closing hour approached.

He was tempted to tell his secret to the young man.
Grinding his teeth at Lahori, the wimp, he thought of
narrating the incident when Shah Jahan had all but fed
him to the lions. Snatching the pen from the head archi-

tect's hand, the Emperor had smeared ink all over the
plan while showering him with the choicest of abuses.
The design of the mosque, grim and overbearing, had
sparked his anger, as it risked distracting the viewer from
the centrepiece—the queen's tomb in the mausoleum.

The Turks and Afghans among them had frowned—
at this rate the plan would forever remain incomplete,
although none were brave enough to raise their voice in
public. Lahori himself, Mr. Ray remembered with glee,
had nodded violently in agreement to save his head. The
Persians in the audience had winked at each other—the
Emperor after all was no more than an ordinary lover!

The assistant had looked at him in wonder, seeing his
eyes fill with tears—tears of joy as he turned the pages of
Shah Jahan's imperial chronicle, and arrived at a painting of the durbar that showed the Emperor signing an
important decree. Only he, Bimal Ray, among the living,
knew it to be none other than the plan finally completed.
Standing behind a pillar on that day in court, he had seen
Shah Jahan gaze lovingly at the roll of paper as if it was
the face of Mumtaz he was holding in his palms. A cry
had gone up as he raised it to his lips to kiss the seal of
approval.

Mrs. Beena Roy treated the books her husband had
started to bring home and his reading outbursts with
suspicion. Privately, she had expected it to be much
worse, his midlife crisis, believing what she heard from
her friends at the income tax office—men of fifty taking
up with young maidservants; hiding whisky bottles under
the bed, or developing a prostate problem. No stranger
to his reading habits, she had expressed only a mild sus-

picion in the beginning, giving him the benefit of the doubt. Perhaps the government had asked Mr. Mehta's firm to check the accounts of the Taj as part of its anti-corruption drive. She had reacted woodenly when quite out of the blue her husband had suggested visiting the Taj Mahal on their twenty-third anniversary.

"Are you suggesting a second honeymoon?" she had replied, using a measuring ruler to beat down a cotton-filled blanket that bloated up every now and then on account of humidity.

"Second . . . ?"

"Don't you remember the first one?"

He did remember his first visit to the Taj, *their* first visit, a good month after their marriage. Mostly, he remembered the journey—no less tortuous than in the Mughal times—plagued by missed buses, un-ladylike ladies' toilets and an overbearing urge to return to their Delhi flat as soon as possible.

"You can take Keya and her mother if you want to go again."

Looking up from Sir Thomas Rowe's account of the Mughal court, Mr. Ray gave Beena a searching look.

It had been years since he'd met Beena's niece, Sutapa, and her daughter Keya, then eight years old. He remembered the mother as pleasing and outspoken, almost as playful as her daughter. Separated from her husband and on the verge of divorce, she was planning a trip north from Calcutta to get away from it all. There were grounds for worrying, he felt, having to save his secret from another adult who'd share the same roof. What if she asked him awkward questions?

"History is my favourite," Sutapa had declared, going through Mr. Ray's books borrowed from the library. Just as he had feared, she had asked one awkward question after another soon after she arrived at their home and tested his knowledge to the full. Keya had played her part too, replacing the evening's reading and folding with a lively Q&A.

"Why didn't they build the Black Taj?"

"Black?"

"Yes. Didn't Shah Jahan wish to be buried in a black tomb?"

"No, no . . ." Mr. Ray shook his head.

"How do you know?" the girl persisted while her mother frowned, and Beena waited for him to answer sitting before a pile of unfolded linen.

There was never a plan to build a Black Taj or anything like that, he knew for a fact. The Emperor was then mulling over a new capital in Delhi. Why would he have wished to be buried anywhere else? Mr. Ray exercised extreme caution, pulling back from his reminiscences to offer a piece of archaeological evidence—the rumoured spot of the black tomb had been dug up many a time, but no trace of any building was ever found.

Then again, he had to refute the story of Shah Jahan blinding his architects after the Taj had been completed so that they could never build anything so magnificent. He controlled his laugh. . . . *he should've blinded that impostor . . . would've stopped him from using his rotten eyes and swollen head ever again!*

"We must go on a full moon," Sutapa had taken charge of the planning, mildly surprised at her aunt's refusal to come along but thrilled at the prospect of having an expert all to themselves as guide.

"We never saw the Taj at full moon." Breaking her silence, Beena had reproved her husband. "At least one of us will have the chance to now."

It was pointless, he knew, to quell the "full moon" fever. Who'd have seen the Taj at night in those days? Besides the guards, no one was allowed to even cross the forecourt let alone climb up to the mausoleum. The row of chinar trees too would've prevented peeping toms outside the walls from having a peek. Yes, Shah Jahan could've entered the complex if he'd wished to. But then, it was common knowledge that the Emperor went to bed promptly at ten.

"It's nothing much . . . just a trap for tourists . . ." he had tried to assuage Beena's disappointment.

"How would *you* know?" His wife had refused to be soothed, adding her own expertise drawn from her friends . . . "In any case it's better to go now before acid rain drowns your Taj in a year or two . . ."

Mr. Ray had turned up the TV to bring the evening's Q&A to a close.

On the day they left for Agra, the day after their twenty-third anniversary, Mr. Ray felt buoyant on account of what had happened the day before at the Archives. He had gone prepared, armed with Keya's school geometry box full of pens, compasses, and callipers. The reading hall was busier than usual, and he didn't have the assistant's undivided attention. But that hadn't stopped him donning the frayed pair of gloves and turning the folios' pages.

For days now he had felt it necessary to correct the mistakes in the plans. He blamed the archaeologists— British and Indian—for the inaccuracies, mixing up the Mughal gaz, for example, with their modern feet and inches, metres and decimals. There were glaring errors in the dimensions of the grid on which the Taj sat. Pen in hand, he had started to cross out the offending parts and insert the facts as he knew them to be true, unmind- ful of the hovering assistant and other visitors. He felt like the Emperor, correcting the draft plans presented to him by the head architect, and adding the finishing touches. How was anyone to know what was what in the seventeenth century, and he was proud to supply an eye- witness account. It took him much longer to finish than he had imagined, and by the time all the folios had been corrected the assistant had left for the day without the usual invitation to tea. As an afterthought, he had gone back over the plans and inserted the names of the archi- tects too at the bottom, just as artists would in miniature paintings, starting with that of the rascal and ending with his very own Persian name.

Their plans changed within moments of arriving in Agra. Mr. Ray had taken charge as they jostled through the bazaar's congested lanes within sight of the Taj com- plex, surprising Sutapa with his intimate knowledge of the city. He knew the quickest way to the perfume mar- ket; which turn to avoid as it would invariably lead to a blind alley; and how best to slip past the pesky vendors by escaping to the banks of the Yamuna.

"Aren't we going to the Taj?" Keya pouted, about to break into tears. Once they had pulled into midstream, the Taj appeared in full view, sitting still on the flowing river, and turned them speechless. This was the garden city he had glimpsed, arriving by boat three hundred years ago! Not just travellers, but the natives themselves went by the river to visit the tombs—the Ram Bagh or the Chini-karauza. He smiled to himself—even after all these years he hadn't forgotten the best way to view the Taj.

"Wish I was there then . . ." Mr. Ray caught Sutapa mumbling wistfully to herself. On his part, he wished to be a crane nesting on the dry riverbed, or a water buffalo left to roam on the banks by its owner, feasting his eyes on the Taj all day. Even he, the fastidious Persian, was astounded, he remembered, seeing the completed mausoleum, fooled by the guile of the upstart Emperor. Where Akbar, the Emperor's grandfather, had used white marble to highlight the red sandstone, he, Shah Jahan, had reversed the colours. In place of the typical geometrical patterns one found on Persian and Arabian tombs, he had used flowers—honeysuckle, lilies, tulips, and roses—and made the audacious move of inlaying marble with gems, like the Florentine *pietra dura. Who would've thought a wild red flower had such power to capture a suffering heart!*

They were taken for a family of three—a middle-aged man with a somewhat younger wife and a late issue. Inside the tomb chamber, he taught Keya the echo trick—a word uttered at the right pitch would hold its sound for half a minute. Trying to draw Sutapa's attention to the marble screen around the cenotaph and the ninety-nine names of Allah inscribed on it, he caught her rooted to the floor before Mumtaz's tomb, eyes shut, as if she was praying to the dead queen lying with her head pointing north and face turned west towards Mecca.

"Is it true a dewdrop falls on her tomb every night?" she asked him, opening her eyes. Mr. Ray didn't know the answer to that question.

"How do you know so much about the Taj?" Sutapa asked him as they sat on a garden bench with Keya playing around them. He smiled weakly.

"You must have a very good memory to remember all these things from your school days." She gave him a conspiratorial look, "I remember some too as history was my favourite." She sighed, almost inaudibly. "Sometimes I feel I was here during the olden times, working perhaps as a tomb attendant at the Taj . . . couldn't have been much better than that, could I . . . ?" Then she broke into her childlike laugh, "I thought you were an accountant, but . . ." Her thought remained incomplete as Keya arrived to drag her mother off.

He woke that night with memories of another Agra. He, the Chota Mimar, would escape from their official residence full of quarrelling artists and architects, and reach the bazaar's back lanes at dusk to clear his head and let blood flow to where it mattered most. He'd prowl the dirt roads and the thriving brothels searching for the special face that had caught his eye in the very first year of his stay in Agra. Even now Mr. Ray could feel his temples throb as he re-enacted the moment in his mind. It was Rajab, the holy month. He saw himself standing on tall scaffolding, holding up the mausoleum's plan and shouting instructions to the labourers when a sudden breeze arrived to blow it away from his hand. Looking down he could see it floating like a butterfly. He had caught her eye then—the Hindustani, wearing the typical blouse, skirt, and veil, carrying a basket of sand on her head—looking up at the butterfly.

On nights like this he'd search for her in the labourers' camps along the Yamuna and at the bazaar. If she was a Rajput, she'd be married to her stonecutter husband; if the wife of a captured soldier from the Deccan, she'd be sick with Agra's fever; if a slave girl, she could be starving. His eyes would glow as he peered into cages of women brought from the length and breadth of Hindustan for Agra's pleasure.

Sitting alone in his room at the lodge, Mr. Ray heard strains of music. Was it the rebab they were playing, or the rudra veena? He could hear sounds of celebration coming from the lanes below. It was too late to knock on the adjoining door; he rose and dressed quickly, leaving his room on an impulse.

Smoke from the burning pits got into his eyes and he stumbled along till he found the musicians. A wedding party had spilled over and taken up the whole bazaar. Men danced with groups of singing eunuchs, clouds of coloured dust hanging over them. Firecrackers set off squeals and shrieks, a few made-up faces peeped through the windows and blew kisses at the passersby. He was taken for a reveller, dragged aside, and made to share sweets and drinks with the rest. Someone pushed him into the circle of dancers and before long he became one of them—face streaking with colours and sweat.

He had crept back to the lodge long after midnight and

turned on the bathroom tap to run on a trickle in order to avoid waking his neighbours. Washing away the colours from his face, he was relieved that Beena hadn't come with them. It would've been worse, much worse. . . . Tucking the blanket around himself, he had sighed . . . *Beena would never have come out with him just like that. . . .*

Mr. Mehta had called on urgent business, his wife informed him, the moment he returned to their flat after seeing Keya and her mother off at the station. From her face he knew she was worried about the "business," but unwilling to speculate. Before he could show her the knick-knacks he had bought in Agra, the phone rang again, having him rush off to his office without even a proper shave. His heart had leapt to his throat at the thought that somehow the business about his past life had reached his boss's ears. Might Beena have guessed . . . ? Leaving Mr. Mehta's office he felt dazed. A grievous error had been made, he was told, on a report prepared by him. An error that'd shame even a novice. If discovered, as it was certain to be, the client could sue them for a hefty sum. In his typically nosy way, Mr. Mehta had enquired if he was keeping well lately and if all was fine between him and his wife. He had stopped short of accusing Mr. Ray of wilful mischief. Given his twenty years in the job, he wasn't fired immediately, but shown the courtesy of a forced leave and asked to stay at home till the matter was sorted out and a decision taken whether to keep him in employment or not.

Everyone at the office seemed to know except the peon who greeted him warmly as he stopped to collect his personal belongings, and passed on the "good news" heard last night on the radio—the new train that'd halve the time between Delhi and Agra was soon to have its first run. He left by the back, needing no excuse any more but out of habit and set off for the Archives, head swirling with the events of the past few days up to the last hour. A part of him wished to go straight to Beena's office to inform her that the urgent business had ended. But then he hesitated, wondering if it wouldn't be better to tell her in the evening when she had more time to think things over between her folding.

He found the reading hall closed for repairs. "For how long?" he asked the sleepy doorman, but failed to receive a proper answer. "Repairing what?" he persisted with his enquiries without making much headway. How could they shut down such an important place without advance notice, he fretted, then asked to meet with the young assistant. The doorman pointed to the closed shutters and waved him away.

Back home he collapsed on the bed, exhausted from travel and the day's troubles. Almost instantly, he retreated to Agra—to a nightmare: a labourer had entered his room to steal and he saw guards lead him by the neck towards him, sitting at the caravanserai with his friends after the day's work. The thief had broken the trunk's lock where he kept his precious mementos—a clutch of jewels bartered from nomads, a saddle presented to him by the grateful owner of the caravanserai, his portraits drawn by his artist friend, and a fine veil of pearls that he had been saving for his bride-to-be. Blood streamed down the man's face as the guards kept beating him then made him kneel on the ground before him. The artist Mir Sultan had drawn his attention to the veil, tied like a pair of handcuffs around his wrists. *Kill him, Chota Mimar!* Onlookers had egged him on and he had drawn his sword, about to chop off the thief's hands, when he saw her—his temptress, the face he had glimpsed from the scaffolding—held back by the guards as she reached for her kneeling man. A thief's wife! She had broken through the cordon of arms and flung herself on the ground, the two writhing together, embracing, kicked and bludgeoned by others. He had thrown away the sword and dashed madly at the couple, screaming to their tormentors to let them off, before his friend had caught him and wrestled him away from the ugly scene.

He woke with a start, a cry throttling his throat and soaked in sweat as Becna held him firmly and patted his chest.

"I thought you were having a heart attack," she said that evening as she finished darning the tablecloth before folding it away. "Maybe you were agitated after what happened . . ." He nodded. He was agitated by what Mr. Mehta had told him. His pride as an accountant had been wounded. What was the use of twenty error-free years, if a single one could lead to such a disaster? But the closed Archives had agitated him more. He had felt thwarted from checking the plans once again. While at the Taj he had had an inkling of further mistakes that he wished to correct on the crumbling pages. He had hoped to see the assistant's smiling face welcoming him to the reading hall.

He missed holding the folios in his hands, breathing

in the pages—the dust, the insecticide—that reminded him of the Chota Mimar, scurrying past the labourers in the half-built mausoleum with a rolled-up plan under his arm. At home, he avoided re-reading the books, worried about an onslaught of unpleasant memories. Would the thief reappear in his nightmares—hung from the gallows as his poor wife watched in horror? Would he see himself sword-fighting the guards to win his release? Or thrown out of Agra by Lahori for sheltering a whore? As days went by he tried in vain to block out his past life, shut the southern window to keep out the howling—his own—down the alleys as he banged on doors in search of the thief's wife.

Beena suspected a link between her husband's unexpected error and his architectural readings, but it was too great a mystery for her to solve. As a whole month of enforced leave went by, she tried to distract him by cutting short her evening's folding and reading out her own manuals brought home from the income tax office. As an accountant he might be interested to read what mockery was made of accounting, she thought. Perhaps it was time for him even to start thinking about early retirement, at least a change that'd take them out of Delhi. She had flickering doubts about her young niece after a postcard arrived from Calcutta bearing a photo of the Taj at full moon with "Next time!" scrawled across it. She had hidden it from him, following her friends' advice not to fan the flames of his mid-life crisis.

She had thought nothing though when the doorbell rang one Saturday morning, and she had to explain to their visitors once again about Ray and Roy. The three men were from the Archives, and she had left them to her husband while she went to make tea.

Mr. Ray recognized the young man and flushed. Improbable as it seemed, for a moment he thought they had come to inform him of the reopening of the reading hall, reasoning to himself that it'd be easy to find his address in the visitors' book that he filled meticulously during each visit. He felt light, almost light-headed after a whole brooding month.

"We have reason to believe you have tampered with our records, Mr. Ray," the oldest of the three, the Archive's director, said, drawing out a file. He continued grimly. "You've falsified the official records of a national treasure . . . no," he corrected himself, "of a world treasure . . . the Taj Mahal."

"Falsified . . . ?" Mr. Ray could only repeat the incriminating word. The young man kept his head lowered; the third, balding member of the group held a steady gaze at his confused face.

"Beyond doubt it is a punishable crime . . ."

"What authority do you have changing the Taj's plans, Mr. Ray?" the balding man, the expert, started his interrogation. "By what *historical* authority, I mean. Can you prove that these are wrong?" He gave a sarcastic laugh. "Prove that the Maharajah of Jaipur who was the first to draw up the Taj's plans was a fool? Was Lord Curzon, who saved those plans, a fool too?" With a quick glance at the director, he went on, "The Archaeological Society of India is no fool either. You've written down the names of architects even, when no one really knows who they were. Might've been a Turk, or a European even. . . ." He ignored Mr. Ray's frown. "How can you claim to know more than anyone about these architects?"

The director changed his tone as if scolding a schoolboy. "Even children are taught not to scribble in textbooks. At first we thought it was a security issue, that the Taj might be at risk. Someone perhaps was studying the plans to plant a bomb inside." Mr. Ray could see Beena standing behind the curtains with the tea tray waiting for a suitable moment to make her entrance. The director shook his head, "In the end we thought it was nothing but an act of . . ."

"Madness." The expert supplied the missing word.

The file was pushed in front of him, opened at a letter written by Mr. Bimal Ray to the Archive's director giving him his undertaking never again to set foot inside the reading hall or face the consequences, and he was asked to add his signature.

Beena received Mr. Mehta's call just as the visitors had left. Cupping the phone with her palm, she had passed it to her husband. From his boss's voice he couldn't tell at first if he was calling on routine business or to convey news. In his usual manner he had gone on about this and that then brought up the report. It was all right, he chuckled, the client had glossed over the error and ended up praising it to high heavens! It was one of those things—a sheer stroke of luck. "Come back from your holiday!" He could feel Mr. Mehta slapping his back as he rung off.

He sat by the southern window after the sun had set. It was the best hour to view the Taj—the saddest. He heard nothing, just the silence of the completed mausoleum free of labourers and architects. Not a leaf stirred in the garden, the river still like a mirror. The bazaar and the caravanserai were empty, not even a beggar stooped for alms before the mosque's closed door. The Emperor had left with his soldiers on a campaign far from Agra.

He saw the Chota Mimar crossing the mountains on a mule as he returned home to Persia, stopping every now and then to cast a look back at the queen's tomb—glowing in the dark like the heart of an angel.

translated from Urdu by Carla Petievich

{ Arunachal Pradesh }—

The Scent of Orange Blossom
Mamang Dai

SHE STOOD WITH HER HANDS steeped in blood. The legs of the pig stuck straight up and its entrails had spilled out of its belly onto the glistening mat of green leaves. A big fire leaped and crackled. The smell of roasting and burning wafted up from every house and mingled above her head in a dense fragrance of charcoal and wood ash. Everyone was talking at the top of their voices.

MAMANG DAI (1957–) is a journalist and former civil servant. In addition to a collection of short stories, *The Legends of Pensam* (from which this story is taken), she has also written a book of verse, and a non-fiction exploration of the culture and history of Arunachal Pradesh—one of the most remote states in India, home to about twenty major tribes, and thus often a blank in the imagination of Indians from other parts of the country. "The Scent of Orange Blossom" channels the ideas of landscape, memory, tribe, and family into a vivid and harmonious whole through the viewpoint of a young wife. The protagonist at one stage thrills to "the green of living," and indeed the whole of Dai's story pulses with a vision of stability, plenitude, fertility, and contentment.

"Hai, here, here! Sit for a while. Have a drink!"

All the visitors were pressed upon to taste the rice beer in return for the gifts of more rice beer and strips of meat that they arrived with. It was the festival of solung. She delicately eased out the liver of the dead animal. It was still warm and slippery with dark blood, and she could feel the weight of it on her wrists as she heaved it into a shallow tin dish. Her husband, Kao, worked beside her silently, knowing exactly where to plunge the knife to extract exact portions of meat that would be distributed to all their friends. Now and then he lunged at the dogs. "Shoo!" He hissed, and laughed, and Nenem knew he was happy by the way he worked: concentrated, deft, peaceful.

"That's a good-looking pig you've got there," said Jebu, a young man for whom a chair had been brought out.

"Yah, he's okay," Kao replied.

Jebu smiled at Nenem. "Hah! Hah! Does he ever say anything more than three words?"

She smiled briefly. Making her husband laugh and talk was like trying to lift an enormous stone. Everyone joked about it.

"Hai! Look who's here!"

More people were arriving. Nenem rushed into the kitchen to give instructions. "You can start serving," she said, pointing to the wrapped packages of egg and crushed ginger. "Tonight, tonight I will see everyone well fed and happy," she thought. She ran out again and hitched up her ga-le tighter. The sweat glowed on her face. She felt the evening breeze touch her bare shoulders. She smiled happily when she caught Kao's glance. They were partners now. Step by step he had led her here—even she could not have explained how—to be his wife, and the mistress of this house that he had constructed with skill and determination over a period of six years. Perhaps it was the magic in a stone, a river, or a song. One could not be sure which.

She only knew that the beginning had been very different, and that though it now belonged to a distant past, the memory of it would trail her forever like the scent of orange blossom.

For five years Nenem pined in secret. She walked in the sunlight and saw the budding life hidden in the cold winter stems and shrubs. One morning the peach trees opened in pale pink blossoms, and eleven ducklings hatched with yellow breasts and bills, identical to their mother's. They tottered and crept under her wing. The drake looked fierce and stared around hissing and breathing hard though he kept ducking his head to the mother duck as if in perplexed obeisance. Then the mother rose and left the straggling chicks and nipped hard at him. He darted away, while she calmly waddled into the garden shaking her feathers, shaking off the long wait of gestation, dipped her head into the tin trough and began to splash and clean herself. Then she swept into the undergrowth in great excitement and the chicks ran up to her as fast as they could.

The green of living! The young shoots of plants, the sun and dew. The living mud, the stirring of worms. Nenem smiled to see the duck's great hunger and rejoiced in her performance and release.

It was during this time, maybe three or four years after David had left, that she received a tattered envelope marked with blue lines and covered with colourful postage. Rakut's father had brought it to her and though he tried to look very casual Nenem knew he was dying of curiosity. He said, "Here, it must have been held up somewhere. I brought it as soon as I saw it. I've also signed for it in the delivery register."

She was touched by his concern. He continued, "By the way, I hear a new band of musicians is going to play something in the town hall tonight. You should come and see it."

"Okay." Nenem gave in because he had brought the letter, and because the fellow was like her own brother, after all. He had never made any comment to her or to anyone else about the times when he had seen her visiting David's house. And now here he was, back from the wars and tinkling his cycle bell as though he had never been away, and still silent about both her recklessness and her misfortune.

When she opened the envelope she saw the photograph. There was nothing else, but there was no need of anything else. The years fell away and she saw herself again, so innocent and happy! She stared and stared at the picture.

She saw David. Yes, there he was, tilting towards her with that expression on his face, but she was trying to see more—the house in the background, the reflection of a windowpane, the tip of the hibiscus bush, and the colour of the sky. At the back David had written his name and put a thumbprint over it. She smiled, remembering everything about him. He was so funny! She remembered the colour of his eyes, like the sky seen in the river, and the weight of his hand on hers, driving that old jeep and grinning happily at her while the whole world was moving and changing. Everything came back in a rush until she couldn't see anymore because her eyes were full of tears.

That evening Nenem took great pains to appear fresh and beautiful. She scrubbed her face until it glowed. She pinned back her hair with a new clip and searched for clothes that would brighten her appearance. In a last-minute decision she put on her green beads and carried her small coin purse.

The small town hall was packed; in just a couple of years Pigo had become twice its old size. She regretted that she had not sought out Rakut's father to escort her, but then, maybe he had just invited her because he felt sorry for her, thinking that she would not come. She was about to turn away when a quiet voice greeted her. It was a man she had never seen before. "Oh . . ." she said, hesitating.

Just then Rakut's father dashed up smiling and greeted them both. "This is Kao," he said, almost pushing Nenem against the young man who, however, did not smile. Instead he stood silently and looked around as if he was embarrassed by the introduction. Then a loud voice announced that the cultural show was about to begin and everyone should sit down immediately and those people standing at the back should either leave or remain silent! Rakut's father was one of the members of the organizing committee and he rushed away, but not before telling them excitedly that this show was "all about preserving our roots," because already the past was being cast away by many young people.

Kao screwed up his face at the noise and harsh lights.

The announcer shouted, the tall microphone before him screeched, and the sound box crackled and hissed through the two loudspeakers on either side of the stage that Nenem was seeing for the first time. She had never heard such sounds before. The stage was decorated with tall stems of freshly cut bamboo, and on the backdrop was a cloth banner with big, bold letters in the miglun language that Nenem could barely decipher: W-E-L-C O-M-E

Two women came out and stood quietly on stage. Nenem stared at them. They were dressed in short black skirts and covered in beads. She realized they were women from distant villages across the river. How times had changed! People were moving freely across the region and new settlers from the outlying villages were pouring into the town. Now the women swayed slightly and held their hands behind their backs as if they were uncertain where or how to begin. There were no instruments and no extra accompaniments. They did not look at one another but they started together on cue as if someone was signalling to them. Their song began softly, and as Nenem strained to make out the words, it became a rising sound, a soft moaning wind sweeping across the land. One voice rose, the other sighed, and the notes fell like waves. It was a vaguely familiar sound; it reminded her of something deep and distant even though it was in a tongue she could not understand, for the women singing were from a faraway place. But the song was so clear, so pure, and melodious that to anyone who heard it the thought was sure to cross their minds that this was of no known language and that it was never spoken but always sung, like this.

The two women were communicating like songbirds. It must be a lament, Nenem thought, and imagined a bird flying high in the sky bringing news of death while the wind caught the soft feathers slowly spiralling earthwards. The song rose, echoed, and wept without any visible change of expression on the faces of the singers except once, when in the long exchange of notes she saw the smile growing in their eyes as they took the notes higher and higher like dancing leaves that soared skywards until they disappeared. The audience was left breathless. It was an impossible music. Nenem felt her throat choked with tears. What were they singing about?

She looked quickly at Kao. He appeared imperturbable in his seat but he clapped and now looked at her as if to say, "Well, what about this, huh?" And for some reason, looking at him, at the way he tilted his head towards her slightly, she understood why the song had seemed familiar. It was about loss, the kind that she had known when the man she had loved went away. It was the kind of loss she had understood long before she suffered it, listening as a little girl to an old ballad sung by the villagers to bless their warrior sons. Perhaps these women had been singing similar words:

> *These were our arrows,*
> *This, our poison.*
> *This, the warrior's art,*
> *These, our songs of love.*

This was her land. She had chosen it over love. She did not ask herself if she was happy.

It was another summer. Clouds would swoop down

over the hills, threatening rain, and then suddenly surrender, leaving the evening sky filled with a strange, wild glow. Kao came to visit her often. He came to Yelen from the village of Motum across the river to board the big ferry that took him further downstream to the distant town where he was completing his studies. He was the eldest son of the Poro family and was one of the first men of the area to be travelling out so far. Everyone spoke of him with affection and praise. Kao, however, never said much at all. This silence provoked Nenem, who began to talk and open up just so that she could tease him and extract a few words from him. How could she have known that the serious Kao was enchanted by her gossip, her trusting face, her lips, her eyes, and that he longed for the heat and musk of her woman's body?

It took a long time for him to break his silence. Nenem was shocked by his proposal and when he came again to speak to her father she hid herself by the granary buildings at the outskirts of the village. She saw that the clouds had drifted down low during the night, and without the sun they were cradled in the mountains and still clinging to the trees.

"There are so many things to share," she thought wistfully.

"Yes, yes," her old aunt had also told her when David had gone away. "Let him go. Don't hurt yourself. You will see—there are so many other good people in the world. Give your love, share your life, and make someone happy. These are enough gifts for one lifetime. Don't sacrifice your life for a dream!"

Oh! How long ago that seemed now. David! She would

never forget him. As long as there was life and breath in her body he would be there with her. She had promised herself that. Yet her heart was beating wildly wondering what Kao and her father would be discussing. She knew intuitively that Kao would be a good husband.

"Ah, what will happen?" she asked herself, realizing now that the true sadness of love is the old, undying image being slowly replaced by the expectation of a new love.

Nenem and Kao became man and wife amidst great joy and celebration. Rakut's father was the one who worked day and night to see that everything was done according to custom. Old men and women whom no one had ever seen before arrived from villages no one had heard of, and the slaughter of mithuns and the consumption of food and drink was something that no one could ever forget. The ceremony was especially distinguished by the presence of Hoxo's father, Lutor, who had come to wish the family well. Old Sogong and his wife sat on the veranda and shouted and joked in great excitement, for they were relieved and happy for their daughter. She was going to a good home—Kao's family had brought rich gifts of mithuns and old metal plates and dishes. There was even a road that the British had built which passed right at the edge of the village. Only one other village in all their hills had a road close to it.

The marriage was also the cementing of wider ties with villages on the other side of the river, between the powerful Doying and Poro clans, and this was an important alliance for the kebang abus, the village elders, who would be travelling there on many future missions to resolve cases with their powers of oratory.

Nenem's childhood friends Yasam and Neyang wept when they came down to the ferry ghat. They were carrying enormous bundles and an old tin trunk that contained everything that Nenem would need to begin her new life in Motum.

"Yes," Nenem said to herself, "tonight I will see everyone well fed and happy!"

It was the festival of solung and the celebration of her first year of marriage. The conversation was loud and lively. Everyone had something to say. Old aches and pains were disclosed. Personal preferences revealed. In one corner some women spoke in hushed tones then burst into loud peals of laughter. The fire seemed to turn and twist as if trying to light up all the faces. A breeze gathered force and carried with it the scent of rain. Jebu said everyone should sing. No sooner had he said this than the company heard the rumbling entry of a lorry that had been hired to transport the ponung girls from the neighbouring villages who were going to sing and dance all night.

"Whatever one may say, we all become like the ones before us," said Kinu. Then he turned to the women huddled in the corner and said, "Now you ladies there—don't be so serious! Get ready to sing and drink!"

"When you get to be like us you will also grow serious," retorted the oldest one of the group. "You just wait and see. But we will sing, of course! Why not?"

"Hai, whatever one may say everyone of us follows in the footsteps of the ones before us!" Kinu kept repeating to himself.

The girls spilled out of the lorry, already making music with their long necklaces of silver coins. They were dressed in identical red ga-les with short black jackets. There were twenty girls in all and they looked fresh and eager, each one nudging her friend as they shuffled towards the fire.

"What beauties! Hai, the young girls are here!" shouted Kinu.

The girls giggled.

"Everyone must sing!" Kinu shouted again, and almost spilling his drink he rushed across to Kao and began hauling him up. Kao was smiling and shaking his head. Then he washed his hands in the bucket of water and stood up. Nenem watched him closely and heard him clearing his throat. Everyone laughed and clapped. They laughed more when Kao started singing a very slow, serious song.

"Hai! Hai! Stop him someone, this won't do!" shouted Kinu.

There was great merriment while Kao continued to sing with his hands in his pocket. Nenem laughed and they looked at each other, Kao still grinning and singing, until Kinu cried out loudly that Kao should be exempted immediately or he would spoil the evening with his pitiful sobriety.

Nenem looked up at the sky. The moon sailed brightly on a ragged black veil and a looming pillar of cloud began to cover half the sky. It seemed to her that heaven itself was sloping downwards in a shaft of light and it gave her a thrill to feel the evening deepening. This was her world now. A small village in the wilderness, the big clouds moving overhead, and the faces of her family and friends shining in the firelight. Yes, a moment of happiness like this! She breathed in deeply, and felt the baby kicking in her womb.

"The rains are not over yet," Kao had told her the other night when she had cried out about her flowers and seeds. Kao had staked the earth for her scented creepers and she was impatient for rain. "Wait a bit," he had said, and sure enough, the downpour had come one night hissing and splashing. Nenem had conceded defeat. Now she smiled, remembering this careful and attentive trait of Kao's. A row of budding cassia trees in a straight row was his handiwork, and he had helped her plant her orange trees in a sheltered grove on the slope of the hill that overlooked the river.

We remember things by little signposts that we have planted here and there, she thought. She had planted the orange trees thinking that she would never escape the scent of orange blossom. And now when she looked at the trees she recalled all the fragments of the past that no one but she could understand. Time had changed so many things.

Nothing was complete. But there was comfort in looking at the green hills and the river that she had crossed to become Kao's wife. Together, they would raise a family, guard their land, and live among their people observing the ancient customs of their clan. Surely these were enough gifts for one lifetime.

—{ Bihar }—

Panchlight

Phanishwarnath Renu

ONE YEAR THE MAHTO CASTE ELDERS took the
money they had collected from the fines of the previous fifteen months and bought a Petromax lantern at
the Ramnavami fair. All together there were eight caste
councils, or panchayats, in the village. Each had its own

The achievement of PHANISHWARNATH RENU (1921–
1977) was to unhook Hindi prose from the classical, formal,
"high" style that was the standard of his day, and to create, for
the village characters of his native Bihar, a rich and expressive
language inflected by the various dialects of Hindi spoken across
north and east India. This story describes a paradigmatic encounter between the urban and the rural, tradition and modernity,
versions of which are still playing themselves out in Indian villages to this day. Renu adroitly shuffles the points of view of different individuals and that of the community. The members of
the "Mahto caste" in the story comprise the lowest caste group in
the village social order, which explains their self-consciousness
about looking outside their circle for help with lighting the panchlight. The chant with which the story closes—*Jai ho!*—is also
the refrain of one of the songs of the movie *Slumdog Millionaire*.

---

separate meeting place, with cotton rugs to spread on the floor and a Petromax lantern, which the villagers called a "panchlight."

After they bought the panchlight, the elders decided to buy the items for an inauguration ceremony with the remaining ten rupees. One shouldn't begin using a valuable piece of machinery without the proper ritual. Even under British rule, a sacrifice was offered before building a bridge.

They all returned to the village from the fair in broad daylight. First in line, the panchayat watchman carried the panchlight box on his head, and behind him came the headman, his assistant, and the other elders. Before they even reached the village, the Brahman Phutangi Jha rudely asked, "How much did you pay for the lantern, Mahto?"

Couldn't he see it was a panchlight? Brahmans always acted superior like that. In their own homes they called a mere oil and wick lamp an electric bulb, but someone else's panchlight was just a lantern!

All the Mahtos gathered around. Men and women, children and old people all dropped their work and came running. "Come on! The panchlight has arrived!" Agnu Mahto, the watchman, warned the people repeatedly, "Get back! Step back! Don't touch it, it might get damaged."

The headman told his wife, "There'll be a ceremony this evening. Bathe quickly and set up the altar."

The leader of the kirtan chorus explained to his group, "Look, tonight we have to sing at the lighting of the panchlight. I'm warning you now—if you bungle it and don't come in on time, you'll be kicked out for good."

In the women's circle, Aunt Gulri began to hum a song by Tulsidas. The younger children started raising an uproar out of sheer excitement.

An hour before sunset people from the whole caste gathered at the headman's door. "The panchlight, the panchlight!" There was talk of nothing but the panchlight.

The headman, puffing at his water pipe, retold the story. "First the shopkeeper said to us, 'A full hundred and five rupees.' I said, 'Look, Mr. Shopkeeper, don't think we're country hicks. We've seen a lot of panchlights.' After that the shopkeeper began to examine my face. He said, 'It looks like you're the headman of the caste. All right, when the headman himself comes to buy a panchlight, that's different. Go ahead—you can have it for just a hundred.'"

The assistant headman said, "You see, he was a shop-keeper who can judge a man by his looks. His servant didn't want to give us the box along with it. I told him, 'Look, Mr. Shopkeeper, how can we take the panchlight without the box?' The shopkeeper scolded the servant and said, 'Are you trying to play games right in front of the headman? Give him the box.'"

The people of the caste gazed at their leaders with respect. The watchman told the group of women, "The panchlight was hissing all along the way."

But at the eleventh hour there was a hitch. Someone brought three bottles of kerosene from the shop of Rudal Sah, and then the question arose, who was going to light the panchlight?

No one had thought of that either before buying it or afterwards. The ritual items were all assembled on the altar, the hymn-singers were seated with their drums and cymbals ready, and the panchlight just sat there. Never before had the villagers bought a thing which was a problem to turn on or off. There was a proverb after all, "If you buy a cow, who will milk it?" Now who was going to light this fine piece of machinery?

Not that no one in the village could light a panchlight. There was a panchlight in every caste panchayat, and there were people who knew how to light them. But the problem was how could they perform the proper rites and inaugurate the panchlight with the help of someone from another caste? Better just to leave it lying there! Who wanted to suffer the sarcastic remarks of the other castes for a lifetime? People would make insinuations. "Your panchlight was lit for the first time by an outsider's hand." No, no! It was a matter of the panchayat's reputation. They couldn't speak to anyone from another caste.

Everyone was disappointed. It was getting darker. No one had lit even the oil lamps in their homes that day. How could they light them ahead of the panchlight? All their efforts had come to naught. The headman, assistant, and watchman were speechless. The elders' faces had fallen. Someone whispered, "A fancy machine has a lot of pride."

A youth came up and announced, "The Rajputs are going wild with laughter. They say to catch hold of your ears and stand up and squat down in front of the panchlight five times, and it will immediately start burning."

The elders heard this and thought, "God has given them an opportunity to laugh. Why shouldn't they laugh?"

An old man came and reported, "That Rudal Sah is a

big showoff. He says to pump the panchlight a little more carefully."

Over and over Gulri's daughter Munri wanted to speak her mind. But how could she say anything? She knew that Godhan knew how to light a panchlight, but Godhan had been outcasted. He wasn't allowed to smoke the pipe or drink water with the other caste members. Munri's mother had complained to the panchayat that every day when Godhan saw her daughter he sang the film song, "I love you, my darling." The elders had been keeping an eye on Godhan for a long time anyway. He had come from another village and settled here, and he still hadn't presented them with any betel leaf. He didn't care about these customs. Finally the elders got their chance. A ten-rupee fine! If he didn't pay up, he would be ostracized. He was an outcaste to this day. How could he be summoned? How could Munri even mention his name? And meanwhile the caste was losing its reputation!

Munri slyly put the matter to her friend Kaneli. "Kaneli—" she whispered.

Kaneli smiled, "But Godhan is an outcaste."

Munri said, "Tell the headman anyway."

"Godhan knows how to light a panchlight," Kaneli spoke up.

"Who, that Godhan? *He* knows how to light it? But—"

The headman looked at his assistant, and the assistant looked at the other elders. All of them had ostracized Godhan unanimously. The whole village was angry with him for singing film songs and casting amorous looks. But now the headman said, "What use is the caste prohibition when our reputation is at stake? What do you think?"

The assistant replied, "That's right."

The other elders gave their assent. "That's right. Godhan should be pardoned."

The headman sent the watchman to fetch Godhan. He soon returned, saying, "Godhan won't come. He says he can't trust the elders. He says if the machine doesn't work, you'll make him pay a fine."

The watchman made a gloomy face and said, "Please, someone persuade Godhan! Otherwise it'll be hard to show our faces in the village tomorrow."

Aunt Gulri said, "I'll go and talk to him." She got up and went towards Godhan's hut and convinced Godhan to come. The light of new hope shone on everyone's face. Godhan silently began filling the panchlight with oil. The headman's wife paced beside the ceremonial items and chased away a cat. The leader of the chorus began arranging the hairs of the peacock-tail whisk. Godhan asked, "Where is the denatured spirit? How can I light it without spirit?"

So now another obstacle had arisen! Everybody was silently doubting the wisdom of the headman, assistant, and elders. These people tried to do things without understanding them. Once more disappointment spread through the gathering. But Godhan was a clever fellow. He could light the panchlight even without spirit. Bring a little coconut oil! Munri ran and brought a capful. Godhan started pumping the panchlight.

The silken mantle of the panchlight gradually filled

with light. Godhan huffed and puffed and turned the valve. After a little while a hissing sound emerged and the light increased. The stain in people's hearts vanished. Godhan really was a capable lad!

Finally the whole caste was illuminated by the panchlight, and the kirtan chorus uttered with one voice, "Hail to Mahavir Swami," and began to sing. In the light of the panchlight all their smiling faces became clear. Godhan had won everyone's heart.

Munri gave Godhan a glance full of longing. Their eyes met and spoke to each other. "All is forgiven." "It wasn't my fault."

The headman called Godhan to his side and spoke to him with great affection, "You've saved the reputation of the caste. Your seven sins are forgiven. Sing film songs as much as you like."

Aunt Gulri said, "Eat at my house tonight, Godhan."

Godhan looked once more at Munri. She lowered her eyes.

The singers finished the hymn and shouted a victory cry, "Jai ho, jai ho." In the brilliance of the panchlight, each leaf of the trees thrilled with delight.

translated from Hindi by Kathryn Hansen

—{ Kolkata }—

Canvasser Krishnalal
Bibhutibhushan Bandhopadhyay

KRISHNALAL WAS FIRED. He'd worked so hard; day after day from ten in the morning (the down Khulna passenger, 10.45 Calcutta time), his tin suitcase in hand, he would ply like a weaver's shuttle, from Shiyalda to Barasat, from Barasat to Shiyalda, calling out, "Dattapukur oil for rheumatism, Dattapukur oil for rheumatism, rheumatic pains, swelling, cuts, burns, toothache, all kinds of aches,

Arguably the greatest of Indian short-story writers, Bengali writer BIBHUTIBHUSHAN BANDHOPADHYAY (1893–1950) combined a visionary perception of man and nature with marvellous gifts in dialogue and narrative artistry. His father was an itinerant reciter of stories from the epics, and he often took his son along on his travels. "Canvasser Krishnalal," one of his many stories that depict characters on the road, is noteworthy for the specificity of its portrayal of both village and city, the mingled realism and romanticism of its man-woman relations, and its superb "folding" of narrative past and present into a seamless whole. Satyajit Ray's great film sequence *The Apu Trilogy* is based on Bandhopadhyay's novels *Pather Panchali* (*Song of the Road*) and *Aparajito* (*The Unvanquished).*

inflammations, itches, everything is cured instantly with Dattapukur oil. For twenty-four years every gentleman on this line has been using our oil. They can vouch for its marvelous healing powers." Despite all that, Krishnalal still lost his job.

Nrityagopal Basu, the boss of the Indian Drug Syndicate, had called Krishnalal in. "Mr. Pal, why didn't you turn in your cash last night?"

"Uh, well it got a bit late, you see. The train from Khulna was almost twenty minutes late."

"Now listen here, I must have warned you a good seventeen times before now. The Khulna train gets in at 10.21. I waited here in the office just for you until 11.30. I even sent Nitai to the station twice. He reported that the train was exactly on time, not a minute late."

"Well, sir, the truth is I wasn't feeling very well last night."

"That's what you always say. I refuse to listen to another word from you. Have you brought the cash with you now? At least that would be some consolation."

Krishnalal had looked plaintively at his boss, a guilty fearful expression on his face. "In fact I can go get it right now. Uh, well, there's a slight problem. I'll be right back."

"Fine. Hurry up."

Seeing that Krishnalal was still standing there Nrityagopal had asked again, "Now what's the matter?"

"I'll have to bring the money later this afternoon. I left it in my room and went for a walk. Now my roommate's gone out with the key."

"And where did you go?"

"I just went to Goldighi for a walk."

"You can't expect me to believe a story like that. I don't believe a word of it. And you know why, too. You were supposed to bring the cash last night just after ten. You've worked here for years now; you know the rules, don't you?"

"Oh yes, sir, of course I do."

"How many times have we been through this, tell me? I can't trust anything you say anymore. I'm very sorry. We put up with plenty from you just because you were an old canvasser for us, but this is the last straw. As soon as the office opens you can collect the pay that's owed you, commission and all. You can go now."

Naturally Krishnalal was not about to give up his job just like that; he begged and pleaded with Nrityagopal Basu, and he even went to see his old father, but it was all in vain. When a job is lost, it's lost. Like a person on his final journey in death, its course is cruelly ordained. No one can stop it.

And so it was that Krishnalal found himself unemployed.

It was two-thirty by the time he gave up trying to win his job back. He hadn't even stopped for a bath or breakfast yet. For the last eleven years Krishnalal had been living in room number seventeen, a hole in the wall in the western end of the long, two-storied tin-roofed earthen building that stuck out like an eyesore on 25/2 Ramnarayan Mitra Lane and that the city of Calcutta had turned into a public bath. Krishnalal shared the room with two other men. The dirty beds were still spread on the floor when he got back that day. Yatin was there sleeping; the other roommate who worked as a tram collector always came home at four-thirty for a half-hour's rest before he dressed up and went out for the evening. The three of them had arranged to eat at the cheap hotel downstairs.

Yatin woke up as he heard Krishnalal come in.

"Back so early?" he asked.

"Early, late, it doesn't matter anymore. They fired me."

"What do you mean? After all those years of service?"

"I tried to tell the boss that, but he wouldn't listen to me. No one cares what a poor man says."

"What happened?"

"I was late turning in the cash. They figured I'd stolen the money."

"Oh. Now what are you going to do?"

"I'll find something else. You'll see. One door shuts and a thousand open. No one can steal the rice from a man's mouth."

Krishnalal had a few coins in his pocket. He went downstairs to the hotel and had some boiled rice and lentils. Then he made his way over to Nabin Kundu Lane. He stopped at a low thatched hut and called, "Golapi, O Golapi."

The woman who came to meet him was well into middle age; she had long lost her youth and good looks. She was wearing a dirty brown sari; her only jewelry was a few cheap glass bangles and two strings of gold-plated metal at her waist. Her hair was turning grey, though her skin was still lustrous and fair. Had you seen Golapi thirty years earlier you would have known at once what she was. Back then Krishnalal had just been recruited for his job as canvasser; the train passengers were easily taken in by his handsome face and his glib speeches. Coins flowed into his hands like water.

One day he and a friend had come to another house on Kundu Lane. That was how Krishnalal first saw Golapi. He was in the prime of his youth and had plenty of ready cash. Golapi was only sixteen or seventeen. Passersby would stop and stare at her, she was so uncommonly beautiful. The money was piling up in Golapi's mother's trunk. From that first glimpse of Golapi, Krishnalal became a nightly resident of Kundu Lane. It all seemed so long ago, now. Golapi's room had filled the other girls with jealousy; she had a smart mahogany chest of drawers, a large English glass mirror hanging on the wall, and a fancy collection of bottles of Maccassar oil that were all the rage in those days. The room smelled sweet from the jasmine blossoms in vases at the windows.

Krishnalal was rich; he earned three rupees a day; never less than two and a half, anyway, when sales were bad. One day he could see that Golapi's mother was angry.

She confessed, "What am I going to do? Golapi is pestering me. She says she's got to have a place for herself now. The foolish girl doesn't realize that such good fortune is not for everyone. Here she is, living in this house with thirty-six other women."

"But why shouldn't she have her own place, mother, if that's what she wants? Don't worry. Tomorrow I'll find a house."

"How much do you think you can spend for rent, Krishnalal? There's a place right here in the neighborhood . . ."

"Oh, whatever you say, maybe twenty, twenty-five rupees a month."

"There's a fine house right near by; it's thirty rupees. Why don't we just move there?"

"Whatever you ladies want, mother. You don't even have to ask me."

Golapi and her mother moved into their new house. The seasoned Panci warned her, "Take it easy, Golapi. Be careful you don't kill the goose with the golden egg. But you've got to admit you have all the luck. All I've got is that old codger Ray. He comes in here and just dunks his false teeth in a glass of water. I've been asking him for a Dacca sari or an alarm clock that hangs on the wall. The dried-out old corpse had been away for seven months, but when he comes back today I'm going to teach him a thing or two. He won't be sauntering in and taking out his teeth as if he owns the place anymore, you can bet that."

And it was not just her new house that made Golapi so happy; she had everything she could possibly want. She had a table harmonium, pairs and pairs of saris, easy chairs, even a record player. She and Krishnalal would take a horse carriage every Sunday like all the fine rich folks and go down to Kalighat to bathe in the Ganges and pay their respects to the Goddess. Thus the years rolled on, Golapi and Krishnalal, Krishnalal and Golapi.

One day, seeing her daughter settled into a life of comfort and luxury, Golapi's mother cut her ties of affection to Nabin Kundu Lane and set out, I suspect, for the world of those famous heavenly courtesans Urvashi and Tillotama. No one in the neighborhood had ever seen a funeral ceremony carried out with such pomp and splendor.

Gradually Golapi's youth began to fade and Krishnalal's income began to decline. Hundreds of oils for rheumatism appeared on the market, slick copies of Dattapukur oil. The trains were filling up with new canvass-

ers. What had once been Krishnalal's alone he now had to
share with many others. Chinks began to appear in their
easy, prosperous life.

Ten or twelve years went by. Golapi was now an unat-
tractive, middle-aged woman. Her old house was gone.
She was reduced to sharing quarters with seven or eight of
her colleagues of various ages. Whatever Krishnalal made
he spent on her, but it was not much anymore. Golapi
returned his devotion; she never even considered finding
another man.

Krishnalal told her, "Golapi, I lost my job this morning."

Golapi was taken aback, "What do you mean?"

"The boss was furious because I didn't turn in the cash
last night."

"What did you do with the money?"

"I spent it."

"Where did you spend it? On what? How can you
expect to keep a job if you're still up to your old tricks?
Where did you go yesterday?"

"No, Golapi, it wasn't like that. Remember when we
made the pilgrimage to Dakshineshbar. We borrowed
money from an Afghan peddlar. Well, last night around
ten he nabbed me at the station. I was afraid he'd stab
me so I handed the cash over to him. You have to watch
out for those Afghans; they know how to collect their
debts."

"Oh well, you had no choice then. Have you eaten? I
can see that I'll end up as a housemaid yet. Didn't I tell
you we should go back to the village? We could build
ourselves a small hut and have a quiet life there together.
But no, all you want is Calcutta, Calcutta. You can't live

without Calcutta. Now how are you going to live with Calcutta? Who's going to feed you here?"

"I'll get something, you'll see. There's no reason to be so upset."

"You act as if you think there's an army of people out there waiting to hand you a job on a silver platter at your age. Do you think you've still got the energy to do a song and dance like you used to?"

"Shall I prove it to you, Golapi? Watch this. Honored gents, this is the famous and original genuine Dattapukur oil for rheumatism. With just one application it cures rheumatic pains, headaches, toothaches, eczema, rashes, cuts, and burns."

Golapi was beside herself with laughter. "Enough, my young lord, you don't have to show me any more. Everyone knows what a pitch you can give. And oh, how you wave your arms as you talk; just like one of those fancy actors in the theatre."

"Does that mean you think someone will hire me?"

"And why not? I'm sure they couldn't resist. But in the meantime I'd better get myself something as a maid. I'll have to fill my own stomach. If you can't feed yourself I can't expect you to feed me too. Ah, I guess I just wasn't born under lucky stars."

Seeing that Krishnalal was about to get up Golapi stopped him. "Wait, I'll bring you a little crispy rice to eat. Have some tea. Then you can go."

Krishnalal sat back down. "So, you think I'm still good at it?"

"Enough already. You don't have to put on airs for me.

You know you're good, but if I were to tell you how good you'd burst with conceit."

"Tell me, Golapi, just a little."

"There's no one like you. I've seen them hawking toothpaste and patent medicines with their harmoniums around their necks. They dance and jabber right here in this alley, those monkeys, but none of them can hold a candle to you."

Krishnalal was red in the face with anger. "What are you saying? How can you even think of comparing me to those fools? I can see it's no use talking to you. You don't understand a thing. They're just stupid peddlars. I was a real canvasser. Do you think I've anything in common with those ignoramuses who tie harmoniums to their backs and sing songs, jangling the anklets on their feet as they dance? What an insult! Don't you dare say anything like that again."

"I'm sorry, I'm sorry. I made a mistake. Now calm down and drink your tea."

Golapi was happy today. It was as if someone had pulled aside the torn black curtain of thirty years to reveal to her the young Krishnalal. She loved his strong voice, his energy, and enthusiasm. She served Krishnalal attentively. This time as he was about to go she said, "Listen, you must promise me something. If you have any trouble with money you must come here and eat with me. You'll get sick at your age if you don't get enough to eat. You don't have to give me anything right now. They need a maid for the temple at the goldsmith's house. I can work there mornings and evenings. I'll start tomorrow. But you won't listen to me, I can tell. You won't come even if you're starving. Don't think I don't know you after all these years."

Krishnalal laughed. "Oh, I'll come. I kind of like the idea of living off my woman for a few days. As a matter of fact I've just been waiting to get the chance. I'll probably even come back later today, sometime in the evening."

But a month went by and Krishnalal never stopped at Golapi's. When things were going well for him he had given her all his earnings, but he was not the man to sit around and sponge off her now, particularly since Golapi was old and had no recourse anymore but to work as a maid servant.

Krishnalal owed two months rent at the boarding house. The manager called him over. "Say, Krishnalal, what about my rent?"

"As you see, I've lost my job. I don't have a penny to my name."

"But you must see my side of things, too. I paid the owner for your rent out of my own pocket these last two months. I can't go on like that. I'll give you two days grace. After that if you can't pay, you'll have to move out and let me look for someone else."

Krishnalal was in a fix. He had no money left to eat on and now he was about to be thrown out of the only living space he had. For three days he threw himself on the mercy of some old friends and with the money they lent him he managed to sustain himself on rice and lentils from the cheap hotel. When those three days were over he began to starve. All he had to eat the whole day long was a few cents' worth of crispy rice or barley, plain barley without even a pinch of molasses or sugar. When he couldn't afford even that he filled his stomach with water, plain tap water.

The manager of the boarding house asked him again, "What's up with the rent?"

"Uh, well, as a matter of fact I was just . . . "

"I've got another tenant. Tomorrow is the first of the month, I paid two months rent for you, and I'll have to pay this month too. I'm not a rich man, you know that. Take your things and vacate the room. You don't have to bother paying me back for the three months rent."

The next morning Krishnalal was out on the street with his possessions, a tin trunk, and a dirty bedroll. It was the rainy season. He didn't even have a place to store his belongings. Golapi had been to the boarding house several times to see him; one day she'd even waited outside for two hours (the manager knew her and was not about to let a lady of the night enter the premises). Krishnalal had avoided her. Now if he went to her place to leave his suitcase and bedroll she was sure to make a scene and try and keep him there. That meant Golapi's place was out. Krishnalal finally persuaded the owner of a tea shop near his boarding house to keep his things for a little while at least. And then he wandered around the city aimlessly, ending up at the steamer dock at Ahiritola on the Ganges.

Krishnalal had eaten nothing that day. He bought a piece of corn for a penny from a Hindustani peddlar who was roasting corn under a tree near the dock. He devoured it with great relish by the riverbank. He craved a cigarillo to cap off his meal. That was when he noticed a young man with a bag. The fellow took out a handkerchief from his pocket and spread it out on the cement surface of the dock. He was about to sit down there when he started fumbling through his pockets as if searching for something. Clearly not finding what he wanted he turned to Krishnalal, "Do you think you could watch my bag for me for a minute? I seem to be out of cigarillos. I'll just run and buy a penny's worth."

He came back with his cigarillos and offered one to Krishnalal. Krishnalal had suspected from the start that the young man was a canvasser; now he asked him, "You're a canvasser, am I right?"

"Yes, you are."

"For what?"

"Ointment for cuts on the hand, surgical salve."

"Do you earn a lot of money? What's your commission?"

"Oh, it's not bad. I demonstrate the product to my customers by cutting my own hand. I keep a knife with me. Here, let me show you."

The young man rolled up his sleeve and showed Krishnalal his arm. From the wrist to the elbow it was crisscrossed with knife slashes.

Krishnalal shuddered. "Doesn't it hurt?"

The young man laughed. "Sure it hurts, but then I put a dab of the ointment on and the pain goes right away."

"How much do you make?"

"Between twenty-five and thirty rupees a month."

Krishnalal's heart sank. All that for only thirty rupees a month! In the good old days Krishnalal had earned sixty to seventy rupees a month with no trouble at all hawking Dattapukur oil for rheumatism. And he hadn't had to cut his arm like that, either. No, canvassing was clearly out of the question. He'd need a new line of business.

The next day Krishnalal left Calcutta for his village. He got down at Basirhat station and walked fourteen miles to his home in Ilasekhali. It was three-thirty by the time he arrived. The only family he had left in the village was a distant relative. His own home had long ago surrendered to the encroaching jungle. It had been years since he'd come this way, and he'd never made any effort to keep the place up. Thatched huts deteriorate without careful attention, and Krishnalal hadn't even seen his for seventeen or eighteen years when he'd last been back in the village for his aunt's funeral.

His relative took him in. Krishnalal had never spent much time in the village before. The people were all uneducated; they didn't even know how to talk to each other politely. They didn't drink tea; in Calcutta even the beggars all drank tea. Everywhere you looked was mud and jungle. He couldn't sleep at night for the mosquitoes, and there was at least one person in every hut down with malaria. Krishnalal tried his best, but he couldn't stand it. As far as he could see all anyone ever did there was sleep. It was too much for him. All day long the villagers sat under the wood apple tree in the small field where they held their religious festivals. They smoked their hookahs and gossiped endlessly to pass the boring day. They had nothing to do; in the afternoon they would shove a few morsels into their mouths and nod into sleep. Their afternoon nap never ended before four o'clock and then red-eyed and still drowsy, some of them would drag themselves off to the bazaar to do a few pennies' worth of shopping. There too they would sit around and chat; at each store they would smoke and talk, smoke and talk. It would take them three hours to do four cents' shopping. The sun setting, they would wend their way home, for dinner and more sleep. The price of kerosene oil had risen sharply; no one in the village was prepared to spend money on something so frivolous as keeping a light burning after dark. They might go visiting, sit in the dark and gossip some more, and smoke a pipe or two, but their real aim was to get back home and sleep again. That was their day.

Krishnalal was not used to such a life. What kind of a life was that anyway? As far as he was concerned it was a living death. The villagers grumbled to him all the time that they couldn't make ends meet; they were ground down by their unrelenting poverty. But Krishnalal was hard put to find anyone who was trying to better his lot and break the vicious cycle. For someone who had spent the last twenty-five to thirty years harried and active in Calcutta it would have been impossible even to imagine the lazy, apathetic dull routine of the village.

Krishnalal looked back on his Calcutta days fondly, how he would jump up at the crack of dawn and dash to the water tap downstairs. If he didn't get his bath over with first thing in the morning he would have to fight the crowds. The people from the goldsmith's shop on the ground floor, the shawl merchants, the tailor, the porters who occupied the room facing east—they would all be pushing and shoving at the tap at once. And then would come another troop, water pots in hand, to collect some water to wash the rice. The three servants on the third floor of the boarding house would be up and hustling by that time. In Calcutta things had to be done by the clock. He laughed now as he recalled their yelling that once had seemed so annoying to him. "Hurry up! It's six o'clock already." "What should I do first?" "The day's begun. The lodgers will be wanting their breakfast at eight o'clock sharp. Don't waste time."

After his bath Krishnalal would leave for Sheyalda station, carrying his faithful bag. Barasat, 7.10; Nalhati, 7.25; Ranaghat, 7.45; Banaga, 8.30; Dattapukur, 8.50; Keshthanagar, 9.10; his day's work had also begun. "Oil for rheumatism, oil for rheumatism! All sorts of rheumatic pains, swellings, inflammations, toothaches, headaches, stomach aches, one touch of this medicine, gentlemen, and everything's cured. This oil has been tried and tested by people on this line for thirty years now and its good name is untarnished." So it would go until twelve o'clock. At 12.55, as soon as the train left Shantipur, the morning's work would be over. What a life! What bliss! The money poured in and Krishnalal had loved spending it as much as he'd loved making it.

Krishnalal managed to hold out one more month in the village. The idleness was killing him; he'd never before curled up his feet under him and stuck his head in a corner like a turtle hiding in its shell. He was convinced that a few more days of it would drive him mad or kill him altogether. The only trouble was how to survive in Calcutta. Krishnalal knew that there was no chance he could have his old job back in the Indian Drug Syndicate, but he was still determined to have one more go at it. He would go back and see Mr. Basu, and if that didn't work he was ready to try anything. He would go look for the young canvasser of oil for cuts on Ahiritola dock. Cutting your arm was a bit extreme, though. At his age he wanted the respect a canvasser got, but what self-respect could there be in slashing your own arm to sell something? No, he hoped it wouldn't come to that. The important thing was first to get out of the village and back to his normal bustling life. Some of the villagers had advised him to plant some rice; others suggested that he plant arum on a plot of land lying fallow by the pond; it had once belonged to Krishnalal's family. They took pains to explain to him how much money he could make by selling the crop at the market. The whole thing made Krishnalal laugh. How could he ever make these clods understand that he could make more in a month as a canvasser in Calcutta than he could by selling arum and squash in the village for a full year!

One day he gave up. He packed his bedding and trunk and headed for Calcutta. He would make it, somehow. On the train back he ran into some old canvassers he knew. They were from all the best firms, even his old Indian Drug Syndicate. They all knew him and they all treated him with great deference.

"So, Krishnalal, how is it we don't get to see much of you these days, brother?"

"Where've you been hiding, Krishnalal? Don't tell me you've gotten married at your age?"

"What company are you working for now, Krishnalal? I never see you on the trains anymore."

"Are you coming back from inspecting your lands in the village? After all, if a man's got property, he's got to take care of it, that's what I always say. Now people like us, we haven't got a damn thing. That Bishbas Company doesn't even give us a decent salary, I tell you. No, just look at you. It makes me jealous, brother. You must earn two hundred rupees a year. That's a fortune! But then you deserve it. We're no match for you."

One of the men passed him a cigarillo; another humbly offered him his betel box. They were all his old pals. What had ever possessed him to abandon them and the life they shared for that kingdom of sleepers? Here was action, fun, money to be earned, and ways to spend it—women and drink. No, he would never leave Calcutta again. If he was going to starve to death, it might as well be in his beloved Calcutta.

Krishnalal pounded the pavement for a good three weeks without any luck. Mr. Basu rudely threw him out, and all the other places wanted young men with long sideburns, clean-shaven necks, smart pump shoes, and booming voices like actors in the theatre. He was past his prime. It was always the same: they had all the men they needed for the time being, if something came up they would drop him a line.

Krishnalal moved back to his old boarding house. He camped out on the verandah. He didn't go to see Golapi; he wasn't ready yet. After fasting two days he made his move. He went looking for the canvasser of surgical ointment at Ahiritola Dock. The man had told him he arrived every day on the steamer from Bali, at twelve-thirty sharp. Krishnalal looked for him for a week, without any success. He was desperate. He couldn't go on any longer. And what was worse, he had begun to worry that he was losing his knack; canvassing took skill and skills needed practice. He'd been away from the job now for months. What if he got so rusty that the young fellows actually did beat him out?

Krishnalal took his suitcase and marched off to Dalhousie Square. He stood on the corner and gave his pitch, gesturing animatedly as he talked. All of this was for practice, of course, but Krishnalal also needed reassurance. He wanted to test his powers and see if he could still attract customers. He wanted to see if he could best those young men, even with their theatrical voices. "Dattapukur oil for rheumatism! Just one dab and all your aches and pains, headaches, toothaches, hand pains, backpains are gone, gentlemen. This medicine has been used by everyone here for thirty years, right here on Laldighi corner."

Within five minutes Krishnalal could look proudly at the crowd he was drawing. One man pushed his way to the front, "Give me a vial. A small vial for me."

In a grave and serious tone Krishnalal told him, "I don't have the medicine with me. I'm from the Publicity Department of Basu Indian Drug Syndicate. Whoever needs the product should take one of these slips with my name on it and go to 106, C. Poddar Lane to the office of Basu Indian Drug Syndicate. Here, let me write out a slip for you. Please take this paper in my name. The commission is four annas. You can keep it."

Five or six days went by. Krishnalal was intoxicated with his own gifts. Every day at three o'clock he would saunter down to Dalhousie Square swinging his suitcase jauntily at his side. People would stop and listen to his performance on their way home from work.

One day as Krishnalal was reciting the virtues of Dattapukur oil for rheumatism, a gentleman pushed his way right to the front. Krishnalal started. It was the head of the Basu Indian Drug Syndicate, Mr. Nrityagopal Basu himself! Looking Krishnalal straight in the eye Mr. Basu said, "Stop. Come over here a minute."

Krishnalal made his way through the crowd. He was unsure of what to do, but he stepped aside with Mr. Basu. Mr. Basu asked, "What's going on here? What do you think you're doing?"

Krishnalal scratched his head. He felt like a common thief caught in the act. "Well, sir," he said, "I was just practicing. I was afraid I'd lost my touch."

"But look what you've done. Within the last five or six days alone a hundred to a hundred and fifty customers have come to the office with your slips. We haven't sold that much in the last few months put together. And this is the off-season, too. I couldn't believe my ears; they all said they got the slips from my publicity officer on Laldighi corner. I said to myself I'd better go have a look for myself. I can't tell you how pleased I am with all you've accomplished."

Humbly Krishnalal mumbled, "You see sir, I knew I could never get a voice like those young men—loud, dramatic, like actors in the theatre—but I still thought maybe I could do something."

Mr. Basu interrupted him, "You don't have to explain another thing. Let's let bygones be bygones. Come with me to the office right away. I appoint you as head canvasser. You will get sixty rupees a month and all you'll have to do is make the rounds and keep an eye on things.

You can teach the young men a thing or two, do you know what I mean? Come, my car is right here."

It was evening. Golapi was trying to light her makeshift stove on the cramped verandah of her hut on Kundu Lane. She was fanning the fire with all her might when she heard the familiar voice outside the gate, "Golapi, Golapi, come out here and take these things. My hands are full."

translated from Bengali by Phyllis Granoff

—{ Orissa }—

Asura Pond

Fakir Mohan Senapati

THERE WAS ONLY ONE POND in Gobindapur, and
everyone in the village used it. It was fairly large, covering
ten to twelve batis, with banks ten to twelve arm-lengths
high, and was known as Asura Pond. In the middle once
stood sixteen stone pillars, on which lamps were lighted.

The Oriya writer FAKIR MOHAN SENAPATI (1843–1918)
was the author of one of the foundational Indian novels, *Six
Acres and a Third* (1902)—a book that laid down a distinctively
Indian template for the newly arrived form, and from which
this excerpt is taken. One of Senapati's major innovations,
immediately visible in the story here, is the use of a homespun
narrational voice that expresses itself through a "we" rather
than the conventional "I" or "he," thereby both impersonating
and ironizing the voice of the village community, into which
the reader is co-opted. Sly and salty and wheedling, nipping
here at the hypocrisy of village social life, there at the greed of
British colonialism, Senapati's prose here illuminates the village pond (to this day often the source of water for domestic
use in rural India) as a space where all the currents of village
life, from myth to gossip, fishing to bathing, the worldly and
the divine, come together.

We are unable to recount the true story of who had it dug, or when. It is said that demons, the Asuras, dug it themselves. That could well be true. Could humans like us dig such an immense pond? Here is a brief history of Asura Pond, as told to us by Ekadusia, the ninety-five-year-old weaver.

The demon Banasura ordered that the pond be dug, but did not pick up shovels and baskets to dig it himself. On his orders, a host of demons came one night and did the work. But when day broke, it had not yet been completed: there was a gap of twelve to fourteen arm-lengths in the south bank, which had not been filled in. By now, it was morning, and the villagers were already up and about. Where could the demons go? They dug a tunnel connecting the pond to the banks of the River Ganga, escaped through it, bathed in the holy river, and then disappeared. During the Baruni Festival on the Ganga, the holy waters of the river used to gush through the tunnel into the pond. But, as the villagers became sinful, the river no longer did this. English-educated babus, do not be too critical of our local historian, Ekadusia Chandra. If you are, half of what Marshman and Tod have written will not survive the light of scrutiny.

There were fish in the pond. You might well remark, "Of course, where there is water, there are fish. There is little need to note this." But your objection is not, strictly speaking, logical. Although sugarcane and jaggery, body and bone, always go together, there exists no such necessary relation between water and fish. If there did, you would find fish inside the water pitchers in your houses. It is not in our nature to base what we write on vague guesswork. We shall provide irrefutable proof that there were fish in Asura Pond. Consider, if you will, the three long-beaked crocodiles lying immobile, with their mouths open, on the south side of the pond. They were there every day. Why were they in the pond? What did they live on? Did anyone see them grazing in the fields like cattle? Or did they follow the path of nonviolence, like the Jains? Needless to say, since they were alive, they must have been eating something. What could this "something" have been? Long-beaked crocodiles are also known as fish-eating crocodiles. Someone might contend, "True, they were eating fish, but they could very well have been getting fish from somewhere else." Of course, fresh and salted fish were in fact sold in the market, but no one ever saw the crocodiles carrying money and going there. When the fisherwomen come to the village to sell fish, village women gave them rice in exchange. But we can swear under oath that we never saw crocodiles obtaining fish in exchange for rice. Thus, it is proven beyond doubt that there were fish in Asura Pond.

There is another equally irrefutable proof to support this contention. Look over there! Four kaduakhumpi birds are hopping about like gotipuas, like traditional dancing boys. The birds are happy and excited because they are able to spear and eat the little fish that live in the mud. Some might remark that these birds are so cruel, so wicked, that they get pleasure from spearing and eating creatures smaller than themselves! What can we say? You may describe the kaduakhumpi birds as cruel, wicked, satanic, or whatever else you like; the birds will never file a defamation suit against you. But don't you know that among your fellow human beings, the bravery, honor, respectability, indeed, the attractiveness of an individual all depend upon the number of necks he can wring?

Some sixteen to twenty cranes, white and brown, churn the mud like lowly farmhands, from morning till night. This is the third proof that there are fish in the pond. A pair of kingfishers suddenly arrives out of nowhere; they dive into the water a couple of times, stuff themselves with food, and swiftly fly away. Sitting on the bank, a lone kingfisher suns itself, wings spread like the gown of a memsahib. Oh, stupid Hindu cranes, look at these English kingfishers, who arrive out of nowhere with empty pockets, fill themselves with all manner of fish from the pond, and then fly away. You nest in the banyan tree near the pond, but after churning the mud and water all day long, all you get are a few miserable small fish. You are living in critical times now; more and more kingfishers will swoop down on the pond and carry off the best fish. You have no hope, no future, unless you go abroad and learn how to swim in the ocean.

The kite is smart and clever; it perches quietly on a branch, like a Brahmin guru, and from there swoops down into the pond to snatch a big fish. That lasts it for the whole day. Brahmin gurus perch on their verandahs, descending on their disciples once a year, like the kite.

Forty or fifty arm-lengths from where the cranes were feeding, the pond is covered with water hyacinths and various kinds of creepers and plants. In the midst of these, water lilies, like young Hindu daughters-in-law, blossom at night; during the day they fold themselves in and hide their faces from view. But the water hyacinths, like young unmarried girls, gaily toss their heads about, day and night, without shame, without a care in the world. The ratalilies bloom at a further distance in the pond. They are like educated Christian "ladies"; they have parted company with the water lilies, but have not yet joined the lotuses.

In the middle of the pond, no water hyacinths are to be found, because goddess Budhi Mangala visits this part of the pond every night. The lotus flower is the darling of Indian poets; it is the abode of Lakshmi, the goddess of wealth, and the seat of Saraswati, the goddess of learning. Furthermore, Lord Brahma's birthplace is graced with lotuses. So naturally, in our village, goddess Budhi Mangala has the monopoly on this holy and beautiful flower. Once a villager swam out into the pond to pluck a lotus. The goddess got his feet entangled with creepers, dragged him down, and drowned him. Since that day, no one has dared to even glance at the lotus flowers in the pond.

There were four bathing ghats in Asura Pond, but only three were used. No one went to the ghat on the south side of the pond, except when someone died and funeral rites were performed. This ghat was a frightening place; even during the day, you would find no one there. And who would venture there at night? Close by grew a large aswatha tree, where, as everyone knows, two terrible demons lived. They were often seen sitting in the tree at night, stretching their legs out into the middle of the pond. We do not know the names of the persons who had seen these demons, but the story is nevertheless true. There were also eyewitness accounts of several kinds of ghosts, who fished in the pond, especially on dark rainy nights, lighting fires here and there. The washerman's ghat was on the east side; two washermen were busy washing clothes. It is said that you know if a village is neat or untidy by looking at its washerman's ghat. Cartloads of dirty clothes were piled up like sacks, and four washerwomen were engaged in boiling and drying clothes. The weavers' ghat was at the northwest corner of the pond; women gathered there in large numbers, since it was close to the village, giving it the look of a haat, a country market. Just because we have used the word *haat*, do not for a moment think that things were bought and sold there; we call it a haat because there were a lot of people, producing a great deal of noise. The gathering at the ghat became very large when the women came to bathe before cooking their daytime meals. If there had been a daily newspaper in Gobindapur, its editor would have had no difficulty gathering stories for his paper; all he would have had to do was sit at the ghat, paper and pencil in hand. He would have found out, for instance, what had been cooked the previous night, at whose house, and what was going to be cooked there today; who went to sleep at what time; how many mosquitoes bit whom; who ran out of salt; who had borrowed oil from whom; how Rama's mother's young daughter-in-law was a shrew, and how she talked back to her mother-in-law, although she married only the other day; when Kamali would go back to her in-laws; how Saraswati was a nice girl and how her cooking was good, her manners excellent . . .

Padi started a brief lecture as she sat in the water cleaning her teeth. The sum and substance of it was that no one in the village was a better cook than she. She went

on tirelessly, pouring out much relevant and irrelevant
information. A few pretty women went on rubbing their
faces with their sari ends, in order to look even prettier.
Lakshmi's nose, adorned with a nose jewel, had already
become red from too much rubbing. Sitting at the water's
edge, scrubbing her heavy brass armlets with half a bas-
ketful of sand, Bimali was engaged in a long tirade against
some unnamed person, using words not to be found in
any dictionary. The gist of it was that somebody's cow had
eaten her pumpkin creepers last night. Bimali proceeded
to offer some stinking stuff as food to three generations
of the cow owner's ancestors, going on and on about the
fertile soil in her back garden: the wretched cow had not
merely devoured the shiny pumpkins that grew there but
had destroyed the possibility of it producing many more
such delicious pumpkins. With the help of several cogent
arguments and examples, she also demonstrated that
this cow must be given as a gift to a Brahmin, otherwise
a terrible calamity would befall the owner. If a violent
quarrel between Markandia's mother and Jasoda had not
suddenly erupted and put an end to all the talk, we could
have gathered many more such items of news.

Jasoda was sitting in the water cleaning her teeth.
Markandia, a five-year-old boy, who was jumping about
and muddying the water, happened to splatter her. Jasoda
stood up, screamed at the boy in foul language, and cursed
him with a short life—whereupon Markandia's mother
rushed in and shouted back at Jasoda in matching language. In the end, Markandia's mother was vanquished;
she slapped her son, picked up her pitcher, and, grab-
bing Markandia's hand, retreated resentfully. Markandia

began to howl, baring all his teeth, and on this note the great battle at the ghat ended.

The sound of thunder lingers long after lightning flashes. The quarrel was over, but talk about it continued. The middle-aged women formed one group and the older women another, one group siding with Markandia's mother and the other with Jasoda. For our part, we are entirely behind Jasoda. After long deliberation and rigorous analysis we have come to the conclusion that Markandia was the cause of all the trouble. He was definitely the villain; his crime was unpardonable. You may scold him, thrash him, or do whatever you like with him—we will stand by you. After all, as you know, water is life, and everyone used water from the weavers' ghat for drinking. Markandia dirtied this water. Would you consider this a small crime?

Now about twenty women arrived at the ghat to bathe. They all stepped into the pond, sat down, and started cleaning their teeth. Milk-white spittle from their mouths floated about in the pond, along with the bits of reddish stuff they scraped off their tongues. We hesitate to describe what else was floating there, since all the women had just relieved themselves in the nearby fields. Even Jasoda would admit she herself had done the same. It is a time-honored practice, not a crime, and therefore there is no reason why it should not be written. Once someone joked that for every pitcherful of water women carried from the pond they discharged a quarter back into it. That may be true, but we have no way of verifying it. More women, carrying bed linens, arrived and began washing them in the ghat; some washed their children's dirty clothing in the water. But, we are sure none of them made the water filthy by jumping about in it, like Markandia had. Unless you do that, how can the water become dirty? Therefore, considering all this evidence, we conclude that Markandia's crime was definitely of a very serious nature.

The Saanta ghat lay three hundred steps away from the weavers' ghat. No women went there in the morning; it was used only by men. During the month of Baisakha it seems as if the sky rains down embers; a hot wind blows and scorches the skin. The dust from the fields rises like smoke from a fire. There was now a crowd of men at the ghat. The farmers, who had gone out to plough the fields in the small hours of the night, had now unyoked their bullocks. Some had come to the ghat after leaning their ploughs against the walls and rubbing a little oil on their heads and bodies. Others had come with a two-finger-thick towel, starched with rice gruel, thrown over their shoulders. Some did not even have a towel; they came straight to the pond from the fields, unyoked their bullocks at the ghat, and stepped into the water. A few pairs of bullocks grazed nearby after drinking all the water they wanted from the pond. Some bathers went into the pond chewing their toothsticks; they cleaned their teeth, scraped their tongues, and threw the dirty sticks on the bank. Half a cartload of dried toothsticks lay there in a heap.

It was not as if the men were silent while they bathed. No, like the women, they too talked a lot. But their talk was repetitive, always centering on the same themes. Therefore, there is no point reporting at length what they talked about. They usually discussed matters like these:

how much land had been sown and where; which field had been ploughed for the second time; how Rama performed the sowing ceremony; how quick-footed Bhima's bullocks were; how the zamindar's were no ordinary bullocks, but truly two young elephants; how X had foolishly wasted a lot of money on a pair of useless brown bullocks; that this was the month when grain would be loaned out from the zamindar's granary; that the monsoon was expected in fifteen days' time; and that the astrologer had predicted plenty of rain this year. But these are familiar subjects. It is not necessary to elaborate on them here.

translated from Oriya by Rabi Shankar Mishra,
Satya P. Mohanty, Jatindra K. Nayak, and Paul St. Pierre

The Whale

Nazir Mansuri

EVENINGS THE TIDE began to swell, the waters silently moving in from the port's inlet to the creek, the cold and frost of the dark month of Kartak growing intense. At dusk, a fog would form, thicken, and hang till late. The siren of the lighthouse on the shoal blared incessantly.

The Kotada village lay like an anchored vessel opposite the village of Vanakbara. And across the wide gulf between them that yawned like the jaws of a mammoth whale came the fishing boats from the open sea.

One of the best known of contemporary Gujarati writers, NAZIR MANSURI (1965–) works as a lecturer in Gujarati in a college in a small town, Navsari. This story, set in a fishing village, with its brooding descriptions of the sea and the coast, language saturated in fish names and piscine metaphors, and undertow of seething sexuality, may remind readers of the famous whale at the heart of American literature. Mansuri's descriptions of age-old trade routes from the west coast of India and his revelation that the bastard protagonist has a Portuguese father (the hero is one of the few blonds in Indian literature) make this a story set in a world at once small and vast.

Lakham Patari's large whaler entered the inlet, laden with fresh catch, slow as a pregnant woman, lugging a monstrous blue whale behind it. A hundred tonner at least, the nylon ropes fastened to the spears in its belly and side were taut and twisted. Its black and blue body glistened with white spots. Fish traders on the open dunes near the storage huts stared at it, slanting sly eyes into the descending dark.

By now the inlet was in a ferment. Lakham, at the rudder, shouted instructions to Atham Hendiwalo, the khallasi at the engine below. Dropping a huge anchor, the whaler came to rest opposite the huts, the ragged thrum of the machine skimming the water behind. The whale struck the shore, pushing sand and foam further in.

Beyond a stretch of wet sand, on the western strip of the inlet, lay the dunes. On them, fish of all shapes and sizes dangled from kathi ropes. Behind the huts, bladders, fins and tails of whales had been left to dry on raised platforms. Lakham's crew and some willing fishermen hauled the whale into the knee-deep waters with great effort. The whale lay on its side, bleeding from the jaw. The clear waters of the rising tide turned crimson with the blood of the convulsing animal.

Labourers came crowding to see the giant whale. Lakham Patari sat on a wooden barrel on the whaler; his crew, exhausted and weary, was still to get off the vessel. In the fading light, silhouettes of the traders clustered around the whale, trying to estimate how much it would fetch at the auction, even as the labourers began transferring the ravas, the dara, the chhapra-chapri, the ghurkas, the large pomfrets, the jewfish, and the eels lying in the thick net into broad iron buckets.

Meghji Bhandari selected some jewfish, large black pomfrets, palvas, a couple of rajratads, some shark younglings, and lobsters, which he put into a nylon bag.

Tall and robust, his face marked by smallpox, Lakham stared at the whale's back, his eyes shot with a brute murderous strength. He undid the strip of cloth that tied together his blond unruly hair and shook it out. As he stepped ashore, lighting the bidi that he pulled out of his khaki shorts, he suddenly turned gloomy.

The inlet meandered into muddy ground at the end of the village. There, at a higher level, were coconut and palm groves. Dragging his feet through a narrow, sandy path, somehow managing to lift the bag over the cactus hedges, Meghji Bhandari reached Lakham's house. Rani had already made the rotlas but was waiting for the whaler to bring in the fish. The moment she saw Meghji Bhandari, she got up from the cot with a scowl, grumbling, La, Meghji, how come you are so early, you wicked pimp, you swindler.

Meghji Bhandari was exhausted, at the end of his tether. He flared up. La! That captain of ours, that accursed, possessed man, he brought us in this early. If that portugis fellow finds a whale near Navabandar, can he let it alone? Along with the whale, he laid the rest of us flat! Who wants to work on his whaler?

"O, so he has caught a whale?" asked Rani, as she delved deep into the nylon bag. "How big is it?"

"La, Rani Maasi, once he sees a whale, he is as one

possessed. He cannot resist a whale, and we others are unable to kill one. We tremble at the very sight of the whale, and this accursed Lakham takes his spear and starts prancing upon the whaler, delighted. The bastard."

Hearing Lakham's name, Rani turned away as though she hadn't heard Meghji and went into the kitchen with the nylon bag. Meghji, still babbling, went off down the narrow path.

After her husband's untimely death, Rani had become the owner of the whaler. She took good care of her brother-in-law Lakham's crew. Lakham Patari was considered a master at killing mammoth cetaceans—ber, hammerheads, malar, blue whales, and sharks. He would give away the young ones and the mantas at the traders' huts, but got the whales, sharks, hammerheads, and the huge sawfish properly auctioned. In fact, he had been nicknamed the Possessed One because of his passion for killing those monstrous creatures of the sea. But Rani found these stories about her brother-in-law difficult to believe.

Lakham's crew often turned against him. Killing the great whales was a highly risky job, requiring frenzy and passion. Only last year, Meghji Bhandari had lost an eye. But it seemed Lakham was so obsessed that the moment he spotted a whale with its glittering black-and-blue-speckled back peeking out of the waters, he could not help but rush for it. Picking up his spear and ropes, he would climb on to the bow of the whaler and thrust the spear into the whale's heart and let loose the rope attached to it. If the wounded cetacean wasn't entangled in the thick net, it would flee, befuddled by intense pain. But before

it could get out of sight, Lakham would have tied the
rope to the bow. The exhausted dying creature would
flounder, beleaguered by its own massive body as well
as the weight of the whaling boat, whereupon Lakham
would jump into the water, reach its hindquarters, and
stick another spear into its mouth. He could do all this
in the time it would take another to merely decide to kill
the whale. Many a time, owing to his impatience, he had
been wounded by these creatures. But his colossal frame
was still lusty and full-blooded, except for a slight limp
which happened once when, while killing a finback, his
leg had scraped through its jaws. It was risks such as this
that made his crew curse him all the time. The glistening
back of the whale seemed to hold a fatal attraction for
Lakham, as though he found some unknown relief in the
anger, sorrow, and frustration of the chase.

Rani brought out two black pomfrets from the nylon
bag and took them into the backyard for cleaning. The
yard was surrounded by a hedge of columnar cacti. Behind
the side wall of the house there were five or six barrels of
caulking paste on top of a chulha made of several craggy
rocks. The strong stench from the blackened chulha and
the vapour of the caulking paste bubbling on it would
fill the air till it was taken off the chulha. At the year's
end there was usually enough for the whaler, and Lakham
sold the extra paste to fishermen.

As she cut and cleaned the black pomfrets, Rani was
lost in her own thoughts. The boils take him, the eunuch!
How he dances while hunting the whales . . . how he
rejoices. But the moment he sees a woman, he cowers like
a green crab, this vile panderer, son of a portugis. Kills

whales. How could he, an effeminate clown, kill a whale? Tell him to marry, and he acts as if he knows nothing. What does one do with this poisonsucker? He makes me so angry!

Rani was fed up. Lakham had killed a blue whale once again. So Meghji had said, though Rani was not sure. Deep in her heart lay a doubt, almost a pang of fear. Her husband, Punjo Bhadelo, used to be the captain of a cargo vessel from Navabandar. He carried lime, dates, onions, and garlic to Basra, Iran, and Africa. He would return at the end of every season, in the month of Jeth. But he had been gone for five years now.

Two years ago, a khallasi returning at the end of the season had said, "That bastard has kept a Negro woman in Africa. Has children from her. Look here, I'm only telling you the truth. Such a shrew that woman, she doesn't let him come back. She has cast such evil spells that Punjo stays on. Have you seen the spirits of the Negroes? Baap re baap!"

Other khallasis spoke of other things. Some said he died in a storm and that his vessel had just narrowly escaped sinking. Some, even from the same vessel, would give confusingly different information. Be it as it may, everyone at Punjo's house had given up hope of his return, except Rani. Her longing would swell and recede like the tide. Punjo's aunt, Ladudakni, had accepted Punjo's death after five years of waiting. My poor Punjo, she would wail, how can he keep a Negro when he's gone into the lap of the saint of the sea? These no-good sailors will say seventy things. The old woman got Punjo's putalvel rites performed. And she wanted to get Rani's dervatu done with Lakham.

Not sure if she should say yes, Rani simmered all the time, like a barrel of caulking paste. It was her yearning for Lakham that made her wait for Punjo. As for Lakham, he did not mention marriage at all. Finally the old woman had got tired of waiting. She consulted a tantrik who declared, "Rani has cast an evil spell on Lakham, that is why he will not have her."

Ladudakni, tired and unwilling, accepted it, and Rani was totally isolated now. No one could hear the scream that resounded from her depths: I will wait forever for Punjo! Sometimes sailors return even after five to seven years. Perhaps Punjo too would return.

The thirty-eight-year-old Rani had a full figure and a dark ebony complexion with sharp features. Her thick hair embellished her broad, sturdy back, like the rudder of a boat. Tied into a knot, it was larger than her head, like a jet black, ripened toddy fruit. Full lips on a chiselled face drew attention. Colourful satin petticoats she wore, and short tight blouses, her full body swelling out in them.

It grew colder as the dark fog spread. Lighting an oil lamp in the kitchen, Rani squatted on a wooden plank to prepare the black pomfrets, fuming at the old woman. That Ladudakni, how she speaks! *I* cast an evil spell on Lakham! Why would I do that? Let those who do so suffer tumours. She listens to banter and then how she screams. Sharp tears trickled from Rani's angry eyes. If that bastard himself refuses, what can anyone do?

The aroma of cooking food swirled around the house. A wintry air blew in through the thin wire net hung across the kitchen window.

The whale had been auctioned off. Lakham received good money. Besides, the whale's liver was his. Lakham sat drinking with his crew on the deck of the whaler. The inlet was ablaze with lanterns and lamps. Lights began to twinkle in the village. Flaring petromax lamps hissed in the traders' huts. There was great activity ashore as more fishing boats returned and the first thing the returning fishermen saw was the great whale. A petrified buzz of comment and discussion rose amongst them. La, it's gigantic! That possessed man will surely leave us one day while killing whales to go press his ancestors' feet, they said, even as they sat down with tidbits of roasted fish to drink liquor on the bobbing whaler. A dour Lakham sat in the dark, staring at the whale, feeling sad and bitter.

Among the crew, Atham Hendiwalo and Ramo Moto, both elderly, started scolding Lakham. "Son of a portugis," Atham said gruffly, "didn't you stop to think? What blasted thing could you have done if the treacherous whale had overturned the boat? You shameless fellow, I was so angry, you idiot, I could have made you weep with a single tight slap!"

And Ramo Moto bawled, "Did you see the whale? It was not even harpooned and this bastard Lakham dove into the water like a bloody whale himself! Up against the whale, you would have been murdered for sure, and what would we old men have done then? Where could we have gone?"

Said Atham Hendiwalo, puffing on his bidi, "Remember the sawfish that last time? Had I not pulled you away, it would have ripped open your stomach."

"Son of a portugis, la!" Ramo Moto said, crunching

away at the fish. "He has become so vain that he goes around jingling the magic beads. I have told him so often to stop . . . 'Lakham, let it be.' But it is all water over an upturned pot. Who listens to us?"

Meghji Bhandari's squint eye careened as he turned his face away, grumbling.

As soon as a finback was caught, Lakham promptly killed it. He would dive into the water, climb its back and sever its fins and tails, and the waters would heave and rage in mid-ocean. Large-bodied finbacks soaked in blood, with fins and tails severed, would be thrown back into the sea—only their fins and tails were of use.

After every hunt, the crew blamed him in a similar fashion. Lakham chewed silently on the roasted bombay duck, staring at the whale all the time.

"La, Moto, hear this. I went now to give the fish to Rani Maasi. On hearing of the whale, she started screaming, 'Poisonsuckers, may you suffer boils, you effeminates, nothing but hijras . . . going to hunt whales. Brazen men, indeed!'"

Hearing Meghji Bhandari, all except Lakham fell to laughing. Lakham continued to look sullen. He grew agitated at the very mention of Rani.

Atham instinctively understood this. "La, come on now, bhai Lakham," he said, "the drinks are beginning to affect us. Let's leave you now. It is night already. And tomorrow is the eleventh day after the full moon. Soon we'll go to serve our ancestors, hunting whales once again!"

And so they left him in the barge of the whaler.

Lakham kept staring from the deck of the whaler. As

soon as the fishermen had reached shore, clambered over the whale and left, he pulled up the barge with the rope.

The tide was rising now. It was time for the night's meal. From the wide inlet creek the floodwaters surged into the muddy ground of the coastal village. Foxes set out in search of dead fish and crabs. The nets from the creek lay haphazardly entangled on the saline land. Flamingos and Siberian cranes settled down in the shallow water for the night. Lakham felt irritated. His urge to go home had died. How she speaks, the shameless woman. So we are effeminate. How come she wants to embrace us then, this whale of a woman? Ladudakni understands. She says, "Marry again, marry, even the eunuchs fare better than you . . ." Lakham was lost in the smouldering past.

Lakham had been a mere lad of sixteen then. That bleak, joyless winter noon, he had come home with crabs from the creek. Sidi Moto was sewing nets on the shore. Punjo was at sea. Rani was alone at home.

Lakham had a bath in his loincloth and came into the house, his body muscular and burnished. Rani had dragged him into her little chamber, desperate, blind with passion. Though physically strong enough, Lakham was stunned by Rani Bhabhi's assault and started wailing. Rani had seethed, lashing at him with a stingray cane till, whimpering, Lakham had fled towards the haunted place in the palm grove.

Some distance away, under the palm trees, a group of hijras squatted around a bonfire. On seeing a robust, fair-complexioned boy, they started to cheer. When they left, they took him with them. This troupe of hijras used to come to the village every year, but was not seen after that.

In the four years Lakham spent among the hijras, he was forcibly stripped and had many sexual antics performed on him. His tender mind was torn asunder, it blazed at the very reference to sex. One day he got the chance to flee, and after two, three days of wandering, he managed to reach the Mandvi port. The captain of a vessel at the Malabar coast took him in and put the sturdy youth to work as a khallasi under the storekeeper. The great freight ship plied all the year round between Calicut, Cochin, Mangalore, and Basra, Iran. Whenever Lakham had some time to himself, he would remember the hijras' antics. . . . Rani Bhabhi's lusty embrace one bleak afternoon . . . he understood it a little now.

About six years later, the vessel anchored at Diu. Only then, after ten years of wandering, did he come back to the village. Sidi Moto was on his deathbed and Punjo had not come home for five years. Like the flood tide at the end of the fishing season, Ladudakni could not contain herself. She sat cross-legged and cried to her heart's content. My portugis has come . . . O Bhagwan!

And now, sitting alone on the deck, Lakham suddenly felt something within him flare up. He got into the barge and went ashore. Securing the barge to the whale's tail, he left for home.

Her cooking over, Rani sat in the front yard on a cot, taut as a bowstring, thinking of Lakham and the whale. In the courtyard, a lantern hung on the stump of a half-dried branch of the huge saragwa tree. Seeing Lakham enter the house in a bad mood, she went still.

Lakham bathed, standing on the smooth stone slab

in the backyard, taking water and an earthen pot from behind the house. Rani Bhabhi . . . the hijras . . . his mind's sky was luminescent with memories. He cleared his throat and bathed somehow, watching Rani's back as he washed himself. She got up abruptly, took the lantern down from the saragwa branch, and went into the kitchen. Keeping the lantern in the middle room, she lit a bright lamp. When Lakham felt an urge to turn and look, he found her gazing at him with gleaming eyes. Her eyes looked like those of whales and sharks in the unfathomable waters of the sea. They filled him with repulsion.

Rani swiftly shifted her gaze. Stoking a couple of dung cakes in the hearth, she started roasting bombay duck, tura, and anchovy. The smell of roasting, sizzling fish spread through the house. Her gaze returned to Lakham's body. He was drying his blond hair. That body with a bit of cloth around the waist annoyed her. Enraged, she drew the hot roasted bombay duck from the hearth and vigorously rubbed the pieces. The fish scalded her palms, but, unmindful in her rage, she started cutting it into pieces.

Lakham put on fresh khaki shorts and sat down to eat. The copper bowl contained a large arab pomfret in a red spicy gravy. The millet rotlas were like the green crab's convex back. And there were slices of roasted bombay duck. Rani sat on her haunches, her legs wide apart, as she ate. The hearth was behind her. Its heat struck her ebony back. Between them lay a silence, like a dead whale. Lakham's fair form had taken over Rani's mind. She was vexed to see that he kept eating, his face long and sullen. The crust had puffed up on the tava. She took the tava down, and thrusting a finger through the crust she said without raising her head, "La, was it a huge whale? How much did you get?"

"Impudent woman, is there ever a small whale? That wretched man gave a hundred rupees," Lakham almost screamed. "I got this much only because it was large."

"Why do you lose your temper if I ask?"

Drops of sweat clung to Rani's face. Lakham was mesmerized by the fleshy calf of her leg. She sensed his eye. Both kept eating, their faces wooden, still sitting on their haunches.

Lakham began to be afraid of Rani. He somehow finished the meal and, putting a cot under the saragwa, lay down outside. In the empty kitchen, Rani continued to eat as one famished. The rotten man, just speak to him and how he jumps up, like a sawfish. Though he seems fine in Ladudakni's lap, he gets meaner by the day.

Winding up her work in the kitchen, Rani came out, saying, "La Lakham, are you making your bed here? Not going to sleep at the whaler tonight?"

He was silent. Without waiting for his reply, Rani picked her cot up from the front yard, hung the lantern on a peg, and thumped into the house.

Lakham kept staring at the dark back in the tight blouse without the overcloth, as though he were gazing at the glistening back of a whale or a shark swimming far into the sea. Just that afternoon, the back of the whale that had been trapped in the nets had seemed to shine at him in just this way. His veins started pounding. Dhak, dhak. Enraged, he clenched his fists. The veins grew taut and in his eyes welled up a terrible sadness.

Rani slanted a glance at Lakham and bolted the door.

The clatter of the bolt rose like a scream and then all was quiet.

Was there a difference between Rani ten years back and now? Lakham was immersed in thought, comparing the length of her back with that of the cetacean.

In the rear room, Rani tossed and turned, gazing at the glowing lantern. In her eyes remained the great fleshy male in the loincloth. His body so tall and sturdy—in just ten years? Rani became restive. That winter noon, Lakham had taken the lashing from the stingray cane . . . from the depths of Rani's mind, lust for Lakham, like a scream, like an uproar, had continued to swell and then cease and swell again. He was barely sixteen then, but had looked a lusty youth of twenty-five. Now he was twenty-six but looked like a mature thirty-five. The poisonsucker had started crying then, otherwise. . . . She had a burning itch to embrace Lakham again.

She swiftly got up and extinguished the lantern, filled with hatred for its steady flame. In the dark her sensual thoughts began wandering like nocturnal creatures.

A howl rose from Dadmadada's temple end, accompanied by plaintive groans. In a short while, howls could be heard from the salty stretch of land behind the house. It seemed as if jackals had surrounded the village. There was a chill in the air and late in the night the frost set in. Rani became suspicious. She had sensed at times how Lakham's eyes roved over her body like a seahawk. How was Lakham, who slept at the whaler even at the end of the fishing season, home today? The thought stayed embedded at the bottom of her mind like a small, pink oyster, and would not come off. Eeyaa . . . eeyaa. The howling drifted in from the distance, now sounding like a queer shriek.

It must be the jackals chasing the hyenas. The silly creatures must be cold, that is why they cry. Distracted by the howls, Rani began to worry for the cocks and chickens cooped inside the farm.

But Lakham wasn't concerned. Tired, he set out for the whaler, to sleep there. Watching the backs of the cetaceans in the deep sea made him feel a hovering absence. Irritation. Gloom. He felt a strong urge to kill those creatures.

He lit a bidi near the lane in Waghra. Just then, a jingling laugh rang in the air. Lakham started. His feet turned towards the yard of the house at the back. The bamboo windowpanes were ajar. There was a screen of net on it. He looked in. Startled, he thought, Don't these people rest even at night?

As Lakham stomped his way through the cold sandy path, the jackals that had come to gnaw at the body of the whale escaped towards the wooden platforms built on the dunes. He untied the barge from the whale's tail and jumped over the whale's back into it. It seemed as if the howling of the jackals was chasing him.

He spread the mattress on the deck, wiped his sweat, lit another bidi. . . . The hijras used to strip him naked and play with him, embrace him, an odd one would lick and even bite his fair body wherever he pleased. Lakham would scream but could not escape from their clutches. The scene he had witnessed in the lane in Waghra mingled with the antics of the hijras in his mind. Spitting hard in frustration, Lakham stared at the sky. Why the hell had she been laughing? In the dim light of the lantern . . . an adult fisherwoman with her man.

Then it struck him that ten years ago Rani had embraced him that way. His body tingled strangely. The jackals hadn't yet started howling. As the tide rose, the whaler kept bobbing in the lapping waters. That night, the jackals struck without warning, sneaking into the farm-yard to drag away the chicken. Very softly opening the bolt, Rani peered out through the partly open door, then took a bright lamp to the yard, closing the palm leaf door carefully behind her. She placed a few stones there. She stared far into the dark as she came back into the house. Lakham's bed—empty? La, la, the deathstricken man, where has he gone now? Back to the whaler? She was quite relieved that Lakham was not sleeping there. She banged the door shut and bolting it, came into her little room with a bright lamp. Had he been there . . . A storm raged in Rani's mind. She felt lonely. Then furious. With Lakham. Her full lips twisted with pain. She cursed Punjo who had been missing for five years. May he get boils all over. Who knows if he stays with a Negro? May he fall to pieces. I'll thrust the grain-sampling rod up his buttocks the moment he gets back. Rani pushed away thoughts of Punjo. The bastard portugis, could he not have slept here? Going off to the whaler. The insult hit hard. What difference was there between Punjo and Lakham?

She suddenly felt it was growing colder. She took the mattress lying on the trunk. Then, on impulse, she threw open the trunk. In the bright light of the lamp she saw Punjo's thick waistband decorated with pale pink oysters. Rani's mother had given it to Punjo at their marriage.

Not thinking clearly, she pulled the waistband out and kept it on the trunk. Then she put out the lamp and lay down. She rarely opened the trunk. Why had she opened it today, why had she looked into it? Dragging her gaze away from the trunk, she looked up. The main beam of the roof was black with soot. The tiles of the roof had not been cleaned at the end of the last year. It would have to be done this year. A thought flashed in her mind. Her gaze returned to the top of the trunk. In a rage, Rani turned her back to it.

Dawn broke. The tide began to ebb. Having been awake till late in the night, Lakham had barely fallen asleep when the labourers brought knives, blades, and whetstones and began tearing up the whale near the inlet in front of the traders' huts. The commotion woke him up. As eight or ten workers tore up the whale, Lakham looked on, sullen. At ebb tide he freed the barge and got down into the water, just behind the whale. "La, you bastards, keep aside the liver. I'll take it later." He spat hard and set out for home.

He was already hungry at daybreak. After devouring last night's pomfret curry with cold rotlas, he went to the shore, stuffed the whale's liver into a barrel and brought it back. Behind the side wall, he put the chopped liver into the caulking paste barrels with carbonate, and set it to boil. He sat against the raffia palm in his underclothes, smelling of the blood and secretion of the whale's liver, and lit a bidi.

Rani had been up since first crow. The servant she employed had delivered some bags of neera. As the sun rose, she filled the glass bottles in the nylon bag with vinegar and got busy in the kitchen, making maikulal with jewfish. Rani could not help looking out now and then, beyond the side wall, outside the door. The terrible stench of the boiling caulk paste came in with the smoke, pervading the kitchen. She came out to put liquor and roasted bombay duck before a glum-looking Lakham.

In a short while, Lakham's crew arrived. Atham said, "La, why are you sitting with the face of a nursing mother so early in the morning? Are you ill? Why are you looking like a dead whale?"

Lakham stalked up to the chulha and stirred the mixture forcefully with a thin bamboo without meeting anyone's eyes.

It was getting hotter. At the yard's end, near the well behind the cactus hedge, Rani sat down for a bath. She remembered that earlier that morning she had been excited on seeing the almost naked Lakham and had felt a sudden urge to marry him.

His crew drank liquor for a while, and then went off dragging their feet in the sand. Lakham, stinking of blood from the liver, took a rope and the leather bucket that hung from a cactus branch and went to the water-wheel well. At the edge of the well lay a couple of broad buckets full of washed clothes, a large pot, and a rope. He stood there, not seeing anyone around. A stream of falling water attracted Lakham's attention to the cactus hedge.

"Oonaa . . . aa . . . !" Rani was startled.

Lakham tautened like a bowstring, something snapping inside him. His heartbeats hammered. He stomped away to go sit in the front yard. He was perspiring, as if he had suddenly sighted a whale. The brazen one! Who asked her to bathe naked? Lakham trembled. Not knowing what to do, he went behind the side wall, covered the barrels of cooling caulking paste, placed the bamboo sticks against the cactus before coming back to the front yard.

She came in noisily after her quick bath, swinging her wet tresses, carrying the water pot up on the bucket. And there was Lakham sitting in the front yard like an owl. Irritated, she banged the pot down in the front yard, made a face, and stomped into the house.

Lakham watched her long face. What do I tell her now? La, did I come to look?

She was drying her hair in her little room. Agony reddened her eyes. So what if he saw her naked? Why had he come running to where a woman was bathing? He must have done it deliberately.

The winter gust made the afternoon even more dull. Lakham lay sleeping in the middle room. He had eaten a lot, drunk a lot, and now snored heavily. Outside in the yard, Rani sat on a small stool, weaving a net hung from a post. Through the open door, she could see Lakham's back. Her gaze stuck there, unmindful of the net she was weaving. Abruptly she got up, went to the kitchen, and gulped down a pitcherful of water. She then came noiselessly into the middle room. Stopped near Lakham, gave him a close look. In the silence that made breathing audible, Rani's face shrank. Was her gaze searching for something on his back? She shuddered, veins taut. Then slowly she moved away and went to her own room on shaky legs.

Behind the side wall a sterile hen had dug up the earth and sat squawking in a long pitch which reverberated in the afternoon.

Somewhere far beyond the lighthouse, the whaler moved. On the deck, the crew was separating a host of nets. As he sat at the steering, Lakham's mind wandered emptily and far. The old men would gossip: That bastard Lakham is of Portuguese blood.

Near Diu in Dholawadi, the crewman of the farm, Bhikho Jharakh, had lived with Lakham's ma, Lakhmi. So too had the Portuguese army officer, Marcus da Cunha. Lakhmi, in love with the Portuguese, was as firmly stuck as an oyster is to the bottom of a ship. This angered Bhikho Jharakh. One day in a drunken state, within the Diu fort, in a dark corner, Lakhmi and Bhikho were tortured and . . . no one knows whether the Portuguese was annoyed or angry. Soon after, the Portuguese lost both his mind and his fortune. He left Diu and went away leaving behind the five- or seven-year old Lakham.

The old folk talked, but Lakham could not make head or tail of it. He bore a terrible rancour against his Portuguese father. Though his mother's misfortune upset him, he would often feel a passionate urge to lash her with a cane. He had heard something else from Ladudakni. She said, "Your ma was just like Rani. Wouldn't fit even into a large bed when she slept. Was as lovely too. But that bastard portugis, your father, the poisonsucker, he was a crafty man." The old woman would leave it at that.

Since then, the very word Portuguese angered Lakham. He addressed the whales and sharks, the finbacks and sawfish as "portugis." And he never let by a single opportunity to kill a cetacean.

They had by now reached the spot where the net was to be spread. Lakham's eagle eye saw a glistening black back upon the surface in the light of the setting sun. He immediately got the speed of the whaler reduced. The crew stood stunned to see the back of a whale.

Lakham recognized that it wasn't really a whale but a gigantic ber. Floating like a corpse. Almost dead. Lakham gazed in silent concentration.

"La, you can spread the net later . . . I'll . . . "

Lakham dangled the wooden stick of the spear, holding it powerfully through the attached skein.

Atham babbled, "La Lakham, it is a ber. Where can we possibly drag it?"

The crew started muttering angrily among themselves, "This bastard Lakham, did he want to overturn the whaler?"

Lakham tucked a sharp knife at his waist and dived in. The ber had a splinter stuck in its white belly. Ah! Lakham thought and he climbed onto its back, cut off its fin. The ber, breathing its last, crashed into the water and the crew started yelling. Lakham again climbed the back of the ber. Severing both the back fins as well as the tail, he put them into the nylon bag at his waist and swiftly boarded the whaler. The blood-soaked finback was left floating as the whaler went on its way.

The tide quickened at evening. The whaler anchored after the nets were set. Meghji Bhandari sat down to make rotlas. Lakham went to sit at the steering handle, his whole being suffocated.

Meghji was talking to Atham as he made rotlas, "Why should one prance about without confirming if the whale is dead or alive? Can you trust the portugis? Remember how the sawfish . . ." Meghji had lost an eye in an attack by a sawfish.

It was the twelfth day of a lunar fortnight. In the pitch dark, bright lights twinkled in the fishing boats. The great beam from the lighthouse began whirling. Spreading mattresses on both sides of the deck, the crew curled up to sleep. Lakham put a burning light at the bow, and slept uneasily, images of Rani tugging at his mind—Rani bathing, screened by the cactus, pulling a face when he sat down to eat at noon. . . . Suddenly, there was a frantic movement in the nets which had been set up. Lakham peered into the dark waters. Was a portugis trapped there? Sitting on his haunches on the bow, he glowered into the depths. The surface of the water splashed sporadically and everything froze again.

The next day, the whaler cast anchor in the inlet. There were whales, sharks, and rays trapped in the thick net. Younglings too. There was a heavy catch of bombay duck and anchovy. Lakham took home the ghurkas and gulali-yas in a nylon bag. Two soles floundered in the nylon bag. Rani was very fond of soles.

As expected, she was delighted to see them and imme-diately started to cook the sole. Lakham went to the waterwheel well with a leather bucket and a rope for his bath. More fishing was to follow after the meal.

Wiping his body, Lakham took a small lamp and went

to the dingy room at the back. The nets lay here. He put down the lamp and groped for the fine nets—a whole new bundle had been kept separate. From the window, where some bamboo strips had broken off, a blast of cold wind rushed in, blowing out the lamp. Lakham shouted, "La Rani, bring the lantern," but he mumbled to himself, "Now she'll not hurry."

But Rani did hurry, leaving the fermented liver of palva she had wrapped in an old wet cloth and put on the tava along with a few turas and bombay duck. Then her foot got caught in a net in the dark room and she lurched towards Lakham, making him lose his balance too. Her touch sent tremors through Lakham, as if he were touching a whale's back. Rani's lantern toppled over on the cold floor. The chimney broke. The spilt kerosene caught fire.

Behind the farm in the salty patch, Siberian cranes and flamingos, who had settled for the night, suddenly raised a din, maybe sighting jackals. In the kitchen, inside the broad bucket, the soles flapped as though they would slough off their skins.

One and a half months later in the bright fortnight of Poush, fishing was discontinued on account of the winter blasts. The whole inlet was full. Boats lay inactive. Lakham made nets and baits. Then when the full moon rose high and there was a thin layer of ice on the surface of the sea, the fishing resumed.

The whaler had been out since dawn. The crew was busy collecting the catch. Lakham sat behind the bow to smoke a bidi. A couple of gigantic whales had been circling in the same area for a long time now, and he wondered which way he should guide the whaler.

Seeing Lakham look far into the distance and tremble, everyone fell quiet. Will this man go after them? If he does, he'll carry on till morning. Will he ever let alone a whale? Meghji Bhandari looked at Lakham with utter disgust. Standing in the heap of baited fish, the crew began guessing the direction the whaler would take. But no one had the courage to ask Lakham. A whale sucked fish in its monstrous jaws and rose high out of the water, spraying some around.

The whaler set off at a slow pace. But surprisingly, the whales were soon left far behind. The crew heaved a sigh of relief, "Isn't he going to kill the whales?" The crew gossiped among themselves. The gyration of the machine increased. Something glowed in Lakham's expression. . . . At daybreak when the whaler set out for fishing under the dew, Lakham had seen a whale splash and the sight had saddened him. The crew too had seen the whale in the fog, but had gone back to sleep rather than tell Lakham.

The whaler entered the inlet once again. Lakham said, "La Mota, the whale we saw in the morning, wasn't it fierce? Its liver would have been excellent, it would have made barrels of paste."

Atham Moto was stunned; the rest of the crew grew uneasy. With both hands, Lakham heaved the great anchor overboard. There was a splash in the creek . . . the crew was silent.

Ashore, the fishermen talked, "What a mighty whale! Lakham is so possessed, he might go and bring it now."

But tossing his blond locks, Lakham picked the nylon

bag and sat on the dunes. He lit a bidi and looked at the lobster in the bag. On the belly of the female stuck a thick, orange fold. Eggs. Are there hatchlings too? wondered Lakham.

At nine that night, Rani thought worriedly, Why hasn't the whaler returned yet? It will be nice if he hasn't stayed to kill a whale. Today, after a long time, Rani had donned a dark blue skintight satin blouse. The blouse had been made a long time ago. Her figure was now fuller. In the tight blouse and overcloth, her body burgeoned, like her intense desire to marry Lakham. Ladudakni could not be told anything about it yet.

Rani put a chain across the door and came onto the road. She got to know from some passing fishermen that the whaler had anchored. She walked on, swinging her full figure confidently. The food is yet to be warmed, the poor ones must be exhausted after fishing, she thought. In the cactus lane, there was a strong fragrance of arani flowers.

That evening she prepared the young sharks and boiled kati in the black earthen pot. When made in a new pot, the shark and kati are so tasty. And these days the younglings of sharks are at their best. Late that night the lantern burned bright in Rani's room.

Rani stood combing her hair. Lakham sat on the broad bed, smoking a bidi. Rani flung her overcloth on to the trunk. Her back made Lakham's eyes ache. She looked even sturdier in the bright glow of the lantern. When she had embraced Lakham ten years ago, had she been in the same dress then? A slow shriek rose from Lakham's mind. Grumbling silently he went to the front room.

Having combed her hair, Rani lowered the flame to a minimum. She lay down on the mattress. Bolting the front door, Lakham came into the house. As she lay on her side, Rani's back tugged at him desperately, like the back of a whale.

Lakham blew out the lantern. Rani's bewitching laughter resounded in the dark; her eyes flashed like a whale's—at Lakham's waist was Punjo Bhadelo's waistband, decorated with pink oysters. Lakham felt it prick, so he undid it and placed it on the trunk that contained Punjo Bhadelo's old clothes.

The jackals howled on and on . . .

Overcome by ardour, Lakham felt as though he was about to climb a whale's back to cut its fins off.

translated from Gujarati by Nikhil Khandekar

Ganesh Gaitonde Sells His Gold

Vikram Chandra

SO, SARDARJI, are you listening still? Are you somewhere in this world with me? I can feel you. What happened next, and what happened next, you want to know.
I was walking under the whirling sky riven by clouds,
with the unceasing tug of gold on my back and the city

The author of two of the best works of fiction published in India
in the last two decades—*Love and Longing in Bombay* (1997),
and *Sacred Games* (2006)—VIKRAM CHANDRA mines the
energy, ambition, squalor, claustrophobia, and polyglot verbal
currents of Mumbai (formerly Bombay), India's most storied city.
One of the marvels of Chandra's writing is how he manages to
sound classical and colloquial at the same time, inflecting a dense
and lyrical English with the harsher sounds of the language of
the street. In this excerpt from *Sacred Games*, Ganesh Gaitonde,
a small-time gangster, tells the story of the biggest day of his life.
Gaitonde's unease transforms by degrees into a nascent strength
and confidence even as the hidden vortexes of power in the great,
pulsing metropolis—the capital of both the white and the black
economies of India, the site of a million dreams and desires—are
beautifully opened out in Chandra's darting and daring narration.

ahead. I was nineteen and I had gold on my back. Here I was, Ganesh Gaitonde, wearing a dirty blue shirt, brown pants, torn rubber-bottomed shoes and no socks, with forty-seven rupees in my pocket and a revolver in my belt and gold on my back. I had nowhere to go, because I couldn't go back to the building in Dadar where I had space to sleep outside the spice-smelling storage room of a restaurant. If Salim Kaka's people were going to look for me, or if anyone else was going to look for me, I would be gone, not found like a simpleton and given a dog's death. Since I had found the gold I had lost trust. I had the problems of a rich man. I thought: in all the world I have only forty-seven rupees and a revolver and this gigantic weight of metal. Gold is no good on my back, I must sell it. Gold is of no consequence until I sell it. How to sell gold, so much of it? Where to sell it? Until I sell it I am a poor man. A poor man with a rich man's problems.

I grinned, and then I laughed. There was a need to find a stash, now, quickly, but the situation was also funny. I sang: "*Mere desh ki dharti sona ugle, ugle heere moti.*" But ten-thirty in the morning was no time to be walking around the outer edges of Borivali with a loaded ghoda and gold, bent by the weight and very tired. There were far fields and thickets of trees and buildings only here and there, small cottages clustered together very village-like, but sooner or later somebody was going to notice, to ask, to want. I had only three bullets left. Thirty or three hundred bullets wouldn't make a difference if someone found out what I was carrying.

There was a barbed-wire fence to the right, guarding a stand of trees. I looked behind, ahead, and my decision was made. I slipped under the lowest strand, pulled the sack after and walked fast, no running, a fast walk to the trees. In the shade I squatted and settled into a wait. I flexed my hands, trying to work off the cramp that came from clutching my sack, from carrying its heavy burden. If anything happened it would happen now. I was enveloped all at once by tiny flying insects, and was willing to take the bites, but they moved in a shivering cloud around my shoulders, a tremble in the air. In the shimmering circle I was remembering the slope of a mountain seen through a window, a schoolbook fluttering in the breeze, my mother's endless weeping in the next room. Endless. Enough—I waved a hand in front of my face and came out of it. I moved forward in a crouch, through the dark under the branches, towards a sheet of water I could see now. A small pond, held in a saucer-like depression, edged around with yellowing weeds. I sat again, squatting with the sack in front. There were no footprints in the soft mud around the pond, no paths through the coarse grass, no man or woman all the way to the barbed wire on the far side of the water, or even beyond, on the road. But I wanted to give it another half an hour. I held firmly on to the smooth rectangle of the bar in my pocket and breathed in, out. I followed the quick iridescent dip of dragonflies on the water. I was determined not to slip again, never to fall gently into the slow whirlpool of the past. There had been a life, I had left it. For Ganesh Gaitonde there was only this day, this day's night and every day ahead.

When it was time, I backed away into the trees, into the darkest shade. I chose a tree and began to dig. The

earth was loose, but dry, and it was slow going, and soon
my fingers were raw. I should have first found something
to dig with, a piece of tin, something. Bad planning.
But it was started now, and I went on, moving the dirt
in fistfuls. When I reached the harder layer under the
topsoil I sat back and scraped at it with my heels until I
had loosened it. The work was hard, and I was sweating,
and when I stopped it wasn't really a hole, just a shallow
depression really, under the dark trunk. I was tired, and
hungry, and it would have to be enough. My chest was
heaving. I tugged at the drawstring on the sack, and took
out two biscuits of gold, and lost a minute or two in the
soft bronze burn of them, under the dappled shadows.
Then the sack went into the cranny, and I scraped earth
back over it. It looked like a small mound, and I scurried
about under the trees, finding tufts of grass to pat down
over it, leaves and twigs. I stood back and looked down
at the arrangement. It looked like an incidental rise under
a tree, any tree, and in the dimness it would pass, unless
somebody sat down on it maybe. But why would anyone
come here, why wander, why sit? It was safe. I felt sure
of it. But from the fence I had to come back once, just to
make sure I could find my way back. But only once. After
that I made myself roll under the fence, walk down the
road, take the corner firmly, despite the plunging fall of
loss in my stomach, a plummet that hurt so hard I had to
hold my belly with both hands. Risk is risk and so comes
profit. If it's gone it's gone. You have to make a deal.
Make the deal.

    All I had was a name: Paritosh Shah. I had heard it
twice, once from a man named Azam Sheikh, who had

just returned from a four year sentence for burglary. He came out of prison and executed another clean job within two days, a daytime break-and-enter-and-grab on a newly-wed couple's apartment in Santa Cruz East. "The good little wife went to the market to buy vegetables for her husband's dinner," Azam said, "and we got her gold necklace, and her bangles, and her earrings, and her nose-ring, everything except the mangalsutra, and Paritosh Shah cut us a good price for the lot." I had been standing behind the kitchen door in the restaurant where I worked as a waiter, taking a break and listening to the boasting, and when Azam saw my feet under the door he cursed me and shut up. I moved away. Afterwards, his waiter told me Azam Sheikh had left a tip of three rupees, after an hour and a half of tangdis and shammi kebabs and beer, but within a month I had the satisfaction of hearing that Azam Sheikh was back in jail, caught in another Santa Cruz East job when a sleeping maidservant woke up and screamed. He was caught by neighbours and beaten bloody. Azam Sheikh walked funny now, there was that satisfaction—that and the name of Paritosh Shah.

Which I had heard again, after I had become close to Salim Kaka, after I had gained Kaka's trust. We had gone out, Mathu and Salim Kaka and me, to Borivali, for shooting practice. In a clearing in the jungle, Mathu and I had fired six shots each, and Salim Kaka had shown us the stance, the grip, and we had loaded and reloaded until it was fast and easy and I could do it without look-ing. That had pleased Salim Kaka, and he had thumped me on the shoulder. He let us fire two shots more each. The eruptions rolled along my forearms, louder than I had ever imagined, and down my spine, and I exulted, and the birds billowed above.

"Don't clutch your samaan," Salim Kaka said. "Hold it smooth, hold it firm, hold it with love."

There was a chalked target on a tree trunk, and I exploded the chips from its very centre.

"With love," I said, and Salim Kaka laughed with me.

On the long walk out of the jungle, under the bare brown branches, through the enveloping thorn bushes, Salim Kaka scared us with tales of leopards. A girl gathering wood had been killed in this very jungle not ten days ago.

"The leopard comes so fast you can't see him, all you feel is his teeth in your neck," he said.

"I'll blow his eyes out," I said, and twirled my revolver.

Mathu said, "Of course, maderchod, you're a gold-medal shooter after all."

I spat, and said, "There'd be money from the leopard skin. I'd skin the bhenchod and sell it."

"To whom, chutiya?" Mathu wanted to know.

I pointed to Salim Kaka: "To Kaka's receiver."

"No," Salim Kaka said. "He's only interested in jewellery, diamonds, gold, high-price electronics."

"Not your mangy leopard skin," Mathu said, and laughed.

Afterwards Mathu stood by the highway and waited for an auto-rickshaw, his arm up, and Salim Kaka squatted next to me, we hunkered side-by-side next to a wall, pissing. I stared at the wall, holding myself, impatient suddenly with the long train ride ahead, then the bus and walk to home and sleep.

"What's the matter, yaara?" Salim Kaka said. "Still thinking about your leopard skin?" Salim Kaka's teeth were stained brown from tobacco, and they were strong and solid. "Don't worry, you can take the skin to that Paritosh Shah, he'll take anything, I hear."

"Who?" I said.

"Some new receiver in Goregaon. He's ambitious," Salim Kaka said.

Then Mathu had an auto-rickshaw stopped, and Salim Kaka shook himself and stood up, and I stood and zipped up, and Salim Kaka grinned at me and we walked over, rubbing shoulders. In the bouncing and jerking auto we were all squeezed together and Salim Kaka in the centre held the black bag containing the revolvers. They were his, belonged to him. He held the bag close.

So now I went to Goregaon, which was easy enough, but Paritosh Shah was one man in this locality of lakhs, and he was not advertised among the billboards for sex doctors and real-estate agents and cement dealers at the station. I bought a newspaper, found a vadapauwallah outside the station and ate and considered the problem. With a glass of tea from the chai-wallah one booth down I began to see a possible solution.

"Bhidu," I said to the chai-wallah, "where's the police station here?"

I walked to the station, through narrow roads lined with shops and thelas on either side. I slipped through fast, bending and sliding shoulder-first through the crowds, revived by the tea and eager for the next turn. I found the station, and leaned against the bonnet of a car, facing the long, low, brown façade. I could actually see, even from this distance, through the front door into the receiving room with its long desks, and I knew what lay beyond, the crowded offices, the prisoners squatting in rows, the bare cells at the very back. The small crowd in front shifted and wandered and re-formed but was always there, and I flipped through the newspaper and watched. I could pick out the cops, even the plain-clothes ones, from the coil of their necks and a backward leaning, something like a cobra sprung straight in the middle of fresh furrows, hood fanned, quivering with power and arrogance. They had that glittery belligerence in their eyes. I was looking for something else.

It took until two-thirty and two false starts before I found my informant. There was one narrow-hipped man who sidled out of the side of the gate and angled down the road with the oily reticence of a born pickpocket, and I followed him for half a mile, and finally came to mistrust his long hands, which flexed and relaxed in hungry, doglike greediness. Back at the station, I watched again, and fixed on an older man, perhaps of fifty or so, who came out of the front doors, stood just outside the gate, and opened a cigarette pack with a flick of his thumb. He tapped a cigarette on the pack three times, precise and deliberate, and then lit it and pulled at it, all with the same unhurried confidence. I walked behind him and liked the neat curve of the white hair across the back of his neck, and the inconspicuous grey bush-shirt. But at the street crossing, when I came around him and asked for a cigarette, please, the man looked at me with such open friendliness, with such lack of suspicion that I knew he was completely respectable. He was some office-goer who had come to the station to report a stolen bicycle, or loud neighbours, he would have no idea who Paritosh Shah was. I took a cigarette and thanked him and came back to my post.

I was crushing the cigarette butt with my heel when I heard her. It was a deep voice, unmistakably a woman's but bass and resonant, she was arguing with the auto-rickshaw driver, telling him she did the same trip every week and his meter was off and he could expect twelve-sixty from some chutiya fresh from UP, not her. I couldn't see much of her past the auto-rickshaw and the driver, only plump arms and a tight yellow blouse, and when the driver screeched off with nine rupees, I had a glimpse of a deep red sari, a fleshy back and plump waist, a quick and rolling stride, all of it somehow wholly disreputable. Now I was impatient. I no longer bothered to examine the others who went in and out, I was waiting for her. When she emerged forty-five minutes later I was rehearsed and ready.

She crossed the road and stood waiting for an auto-rickshaw, one large hand on her hip and the other waving imperiously at every blaring one that passed. I took a breath and stepped closer, and saw under the sweep of hennaed hair her pouchy cheeks, strong eyebrows, large lotus-shaped gold earrings. She was old, older, marked by time, forty years, or fifty, far from youth. I liked her tubby, forward-leaning stance, her feet wide apart and strong. Her pallu hung carelessly from her shoulder, not very modest at all.

"The rickshaws are all full at this time," I said.

"Go away, boy. I'm not a randi," she growled. "Although you don't look like you could afford one."

I hadn't thought she had looked at me yet. "I'm not looking for a randi."

"So you say." Now she turned her face to me, and her eyes bulged slightly out, not ugly but unusual, it made her face precarious, ready to fall on the world with some jolting surprise. "What do you want, then?"

"I have a question to ask you."

"Why would I answer?"

"I need help."

"You look as if you do. You can't get your pants open and you want me to pull it out for you. Why should I get my hands dirty? Do I look like your mother to you?"

I laughed, and knew my teeth had bared. "No, you don't. Not even a little bit. But still you might help."

An auto-rickshaw going the other way slowed and came curvetting across the road towards us. The woman took hold of the iron bar above its meter before it stopped, and swung herself into the seat. "Go," she said to the driver.

"Paritosh Shah," I said, hunching my shoulders and leaning forward into the rickshaw. Now I had her attention.

"What about him?"

"I need to find him."

"You need to?"

"Yes."

She slipped forward on the seat, and gave me fully the blank threat of her gaze. "You look too dirty to be a khabari. They try to look clean and trustworthy."

"I'm not," I said. "I wouldn't know who to inform to."

"Get in," she said. She made room on the cracked red rexine, gave instructions to the auto-rickshaw driver and we went putt-putting away through unfamiliar lanes. The buildings came closer to each other now, jammed together wall against wall, and the streets were close with people who stepped aside for the auto to pass. I peered out on the left, and then through the oval window in the canvas at the rear.

"Calm down," the woman said. "You're safe. If I wanted to harm you, that big ghoda in your pants wouldn't save you."

I looked down. I had been holding the revolver through stained blue cloth. I let go of it and massaged my right hand with the other. "I've never been here before," I said.

"I know," she said. She leaned over to me. "What's your name?"

"My name is Ganesh. And yours?"

"I am Kanta Bai. What do you have for Paritosh Shah?"

I said, close to her ear, "I have gold." I came closer. "Biscuits."

"Be quiet, Ganesh, until we get out of the auto."

The auto stopped on a busy bazaar square full of wholesale clothing shops, and she led me through rapid turns in narrowing lanes. She was known well here, and people passing greeted her by name, but she hurried by without a pause. At the end of a lane there was a wall with a break in it, a jagged hole lined with shattered bricks, and on the other side there was a basti. I watched my feet and followed her rapid walk. The shacks were closer now, and in some places the pucca buildings were so close to each other across the lane that it was like walking through a tunnel. Men and women and children stood aside to let Kanta Bai pass. There were boys, young men, sitting on ledges and in doorways and I felt their eyes on my neck, and I kept my back straight and kept close to Kanta Bai.

I smelt the overpowering round richness of gur first, and then the vomit. We turned right and passed by a low doorway, and I saw metal tables, and men sitting around them drinking. A boy put a plate with two boiled eggs down on the table nearest the entrance, and his customer shook out the last milky drops from a glass into his mouth. Kanta Bai angled around the side of the building, and the whine of an electric turbine deepened its pitch. She left me in a dark room filled to the ceiling with sacks of gur.

"Wait here," she said, and so I waited.

The warm smell settled on my shoulders, brown as river-bottom earth. Through the unceasing grind of the motor I could hear the highest notes from a radio in the front room, the bar, just the tinny tops of the song, coming to me like froth, and I wondered about the quality of Kanta Bai's product. There had been customers enough, maybe twenty on a workday afternoon, sipping steadily at the eight- and ten-rupee glasses of saadi and satrangi they distilled in the back. It was a good business, raw materials cheap and legally available, overheads low. And the demand for good desi liquor was steady and constant, as continuous and vast as the tramp of feet in the lanes outside. I leaned forward and through the curtained doorway I could see just the bare feet of Kanta Bai's workers and the dragging bottoms of sacks, and occasionally the round gleam of bottles. I recognized her sari, and so was able to turn away and be standing at the furthest end of the room when she turned aside the curtain. When I saw her eyes, burning white despite the sloughy darkness of the gur sacks, I was afraid.

"I spoke to Paritosh Shah on the phone," she said.

I was unable to speak, buried by the abrupt terror of being alone, inexperienced, alone with gold. I nodded, and in the same motion leaned my shoulder against the doorway, very casual. I put a hand on my hip and nodded again.

Kanta Bai was faintly amused. A very small ripple of pleasure passed through her jaw, and she said, "Let's see your gold."

I nodded. I was still very unsafe, queasy inside, but this was necessary. I groped in my right pocket, moved the bars to my left hand, and held them out, two of them weighty in my palm.

Kanta Bai took the bars, tested their heft and weight, and gave them back to me. Her eyes were steady on my face. "He'll see you now. I'll have one of my boys take you."

"Good," I said, now able to find my voice and confidence. The biscuits went back to my pocket, and I fumbled out a thin roll of notes, and fanned them out.

"You can't pay me."

"What?"

"How much do you have?"

I turned my hand to the side, to the light. "Thirty-nine rupees."

At this she gurgled out a laugh, and her cheeks bunched

and her eyes squeezed almost shut. "Bachcha, go and meet Paritosh Shah. He'll owe me a favour if things go well. Thirty-nine rupees doesn't make you Raja Bhoj of Bumbai."

"I'll owe a favour, too," I said. "If things go well."

"Very smart," she said. "Maybe you're a good boy after all."

Paritosh Shah was a family man. I waited for him on a second-floor hallway, near a staircase that exhaled occasional blasts of sharp urine-stink. The building was six storeys tall and ancient, with a bamboo framework roped and nailed to its tottering façade, and worrisome gaps in the ornate scrollwork on the balconies. The second floor was full of male Shahs, who passed by where Kanta Bai's boy had left me on the landing, and they called each other Chachu and Mamu and Bhai, and ignored me entirely. They walked by my dirty shirt and ragged trousers with the barest of glances. They were a flashy, gold-ringed lot who wore mostly white safari suits. I could see their white shoes and white chappals lined up in untidy rows near the uniformed guard at the door. Somewhere inside was the sanctum of Paritosh Shah, guarded by a hoary old muchchad perched on a stool with an absurdly long-barrelled shotgun. He wore a blue uniform with yellow braid, and his moustache was enormous and curved at the ends. After twenty minutes of passing Shahs and piss-stench, I was starting to feel quite insulted, and somehow my resentment focused itself on the ammunition belt the old man wore around his chest, on its cracked leather and three cylindrical red cartridges. I imagined pulling my revolver and putting a hole in the centre of the ammunition belt, just above the saggy stomach. It was an absurd thought, but there was satisfaction in it.

Ten minutes more went by, and that was enough. It was either now or the bullet to his chest. I had a pulsing headache. "Listen, mamu," I said to the guard, who was now investigating his left ear with a pencil stub. "Tell Paritosh Shah I came to do business, not to stand out here and smell his latrine."

"What?" The pencil came out. "What?"

"Tell Paritosh Shah I'm gone. Gone elsewhere. His loss."

"Wait, wait." The old man leaned back and pointed his moustachios through the doorway. "Badriya, come and see what this fellow is saying."

Badriya came, and he was younger by much, and very tall, a quiet-moving muscle-builder, with a deliberate padding way about him in his bare feet. He stood in the doorway with his arms hanging away from his chest, and I was sure he had a weapon tucked away in the small of his back, under the black bush-shirt. "Is there a problem?"

It was a challenge, no question about it, and the man was blank-faced and hard, but I was riding now on the thin-drawn craziness of the moment, on the exhaustion from the long day and the bracing leap of anger.

"Yes, problem," I said. "I'm tired of waiting for your maderchod Paritosh Shah."

The old man bristled and started to climb down from his stool, but Badriya spoke quietly. "He's a busy man."

"So am I."

"Are you?"

"I am."

And that was all it took. The guard had panic in his shoulders. His grip on the shotgun was clumsy, far up the stock, and with one leg on the ground and the other on a crossbar of the stool he was tilted wrong and unbalanced. I watched him and I watched Badriya. It was absurd to be near death in a sudden moment in a grimy corridor with nostrils full, unreasonable to be almost moneyed and not yet, ludicrous to be Ganesh Gaitonde, poor in the city and standing to the side always, there was no sense in any of it and so there was an exulting eagerness in me, a glad and crazy courage. Here. Now. Here I am. What of it?

Badriya raised his left hand slowly. "All right," he said. "I'll go and see if he's free now."

I shrugged. "Okay," I said, liking the English word, one of the very few I knew then. "Okay. I'll wait."

I grinned at the muchchad for the next few minutes, frightening the old man more and more, setting his hands trembling on the shotgun. By the time Badriya appeared again, I was sure I could stare the ancient soldier and his martial whiskers straight into a heart attack. But there was business to be done.

"Come," Badriya said, and I pulled off my shoes and followed.

The annexe led into a warren of hallways lined with identical black doors.

"Raise your arms," Badriya said. I nodded, and raised the front of my shirt, and sucked in my stomach as Badriya gently took up my revolver. Badriya gave it a professional flip back-and-forth of the wrist, looking along its barrel.

He raised it to his nose, intent. He was barrel-chested, heavy-necked. "Been fired not too long ago," he said.

"Yes," I said.

Badriya reversed the revolver in his hand, and although I couldn't tell quite how it was done, it was a very stylish move.

"Turn around," Badriya said. He patted me down quickly, with a series of fluttering taps under my arms and up my thighs, and no more than a very slight pause on the bars in the pockets. It was professionally done, no animosity, and I thought better of Paritosh Shah for having Badriya on his team. "Last door on the left," Badriya said with the last pat.

Paritosh Shah was lying on his side on a white gadda, propped up on a round pillow. The room was quite bare, panelled brown walls, smooth and shiny, with frosted white glass high up near the ceiling, all of it air-conditioned to a chill that I found instantly painful. There was a tidy row of three black phones next to the gadda. Paritosh Shah was very relaxed, and he raised a languid hand at a low stool.

"Sit," he said. I sat, aware of Badriya behind and to the left, and the small click of the black door as it shut. "You're the boy," Paritosh Shah said. He wasn't very old himself, maybe six, seven, at most ten years older than I was, but he had an air of tremendous and weary confidence. "Name?" he said, and somehow his limp drape on the soft gadda, his one leg bent under, his stillness, all of it warned, don't try and fool me, boy.

"Ganesh."

"You're a rash lad, Ganesh. Ganesh what?"

"Ganesh Gaitonde."

"You're not a Bombay original. Ganesh Gaitonde from where?"

"Doesn't matter." I leaned back and brought out two bars. I laid them side by side on the edge of Paritosh Shah's gadda.

"You could've tried selling those to any Marwari jeweller. Why come to me?"

"I want a fair price. And I can get you more."

"How much more?"

"Many more. If I get a fair price for these."

Paritosh Shah tilted, toppling upright like a child's doll with a weight in the bottom. I saw then that he had thin arms and shoulders, but a round ball of a stomach that he folded his hands over. "Fiftygram biscuits. If they check out, seven thousand rupees each."

"Market price is fifteen thousand for fifty grams."

"That's the market price. This is why gold gets smuggled."

"Below half is too much below. Thirteen thousand."

"Ten. That's as much as I can do."

"Twelve."

"Eleven."

I nodded. "Done."

Paritosh Shah whispered into one of the black phones, and with his free hand he held out a silver box filled with silver-flecked paan and supari and elaichi. I shook my head. Money is what I wanted, money to hold and grasp, money in my pocket, I wanted thick wads of notes, the thickness enough for silver boxes, for soft gaddas and red bedspreads and record players and clean bathrooms and love, enough crisp paper for confidence and safety and life. My mouth was dry. I gripped my hands together tightly, and held them hard against each other through the discreet knock on the door, and then as it shut and Badriya put down a small scale and two stacks of currency, one fat and one thin.

"Just to check," Paritosh Shah said. And he picked up the bars one by one, by the fingertips, and laid them on the scale against precise little weights. "Fine." He smiled. "Very fine."

He was looking at me expectantly. The money lay on the gadda, and I moved my will like a vibrating steel spring and stilled myself and showed no sign of noticing it until Paritosh Shah stretched out slim fingers to slide the stack forward two inches. So I took it, with a hand that shook only slightly.

I stood up. The room swayed, the frosty oblongs of white light dipped into my eyes and there was a blinking flash of white sky, no horizon.

Then Paritosh Shah said, "You don't talk very much."

"I'll talk more next time."

Badriya had the door open, and the corridor was long, and I emerged from it with my cash in my pocket and dizziness tamped firmly down. I bent over easily to pull on my shoes, and when I came up I had the thin curl of thirty-nine rupees in my left hand. I tucked it behind the old guard's ammunition belt, put it in firmly with an extra little polishing motion on the leather. "Here, mamu," I said. "And next time I come, don't keep me standing outside."

The man stuttered, and Badriya laughed out loud. He held out the revolver, and raised an eyebrow. "You kept one gold bar back."

I checked my chambers with a quick motion of my wrist, crisp as I could make it. "That one's not for sale," I said.

"Why?"

I laid away the revolver, and raised a hand in farewell. "Not everything is."

On the street outside, I was still very alert. I stood in front of a Bata store and watched the glass on the shoe display, looking for lurkers. The chances were high that I was being followed, that Paritosh Shah had made his swift calculations and sent out someone, perhaps Badriya, to shadow and discover, to uncover much gold. It was only logical. But no reflected pursuers appeared, and I left the window and wandered, ambling slowly and pausing often behind blind corners to watch the faces that passed. I was ready but relaxed, at home in these city streets like I had never been. I felt a lordly compassion for the pretty little bungalows I was walking by now, lit up in the soft evening twilight, for the happy, rich children I could see running in and out. None of it was alien now. And I tried hard to resist comfort, to keep alive the sharp edge of distrust against the euphoria of a profitable deal, the ecstasy of flinging out into the world one throw of dice that rolled fluently to the inevitable condition of victory. Don't be careless. Watch, watch. The numbers fell right but the board moves. What is white will be black. Climb high and fast and the long snakes lie waiting. Play the game.

I stood in front of a temple. I looked left and right and had no idea of how I had got there. There were apartment buildings on one side of the road, lower constructions on the other, the sloping tiled roofs of mill workers, shipping clerks, postmen. The temple stood at a corner, and it must have been the reverberating pealing of the bell that had drawn me to the courtyard, under the high saffron peak of its roof. I leant on a pillar and checked again for followers, for lethal shadows amidst the auto-rickshaws and Ambassadors. If they were out there, smelling of malice and greed, the temple was as good a place as any to wait them out. I had no use for temples, I despised incense and comfortable lies and piety, I did not believe in gods or goddesses, but here was a haven. I took off my shoes and went in. The worshippers sat cross-legged on the smooth floor, crowded together through the length of the long hall. The walls were an austere white, lit up by tube-lights, but the dark heads swayed in a field of bright saris, purple and shining green and blue and deep red, all the way to the orange statue of Hanuman flying, suavely holding the mountain above his head. I found a place against the back wall and sat, instantly comfortable with my feet tucked in under. A man in saffron robes sat on a dais in front of Hanuman, and his discourse came easily and strongly to me, that old story about Bali and Sugreev, the conflict, the challenge, the duel, with the ambushing god waiting in the woods. I knew the turns and tricks well, and I nodded along with the old action and the rhythms of the lesson. When the priest recited couplets, holding out both his arms, the congregation chanted behind him and the women's voices rose high

in the hall. The arrow flew and Bali lay writhing on the
ground, pierced, his heels scraping the forest floor, and I
raised my knees and rested my head on them, and I was
comfortable.

I awoke to the shaking of the saffron-robed priest.
"Beta," he said, "time to go home." He had white hair and
an impish face. "Time for lock-up here. Hanuman-ji has
to go to sleep."

I rubbed the crick from my neck, hard. "Yes. I'll go." I
was the last one in the hall.

"Hanuman-ji understands. You were tired. Worked
long. He sees everything."

"Sure," I said. What fantastic stories the old and the
weak tell to each other, I thought. I stretched out my legs,
stood and stumbled to the locked donation box in front
of Hanuman. Peeling off a five-hundred rupee note from
the thinner wad, I remembered that I hadn't counted the
notes when Paritosh Shah had given them. Amateur-like
and not to be done again. I slipped the money into the
slit, and found the priest ready to my right with a thali
full of prasad. I held out my cupped right hand, and ate
the small sugary peda on the way out. My mouth flooded
painfully with saliva, and I was rested, and life was very
sweet.

Now there was no multitude for assassins to hide in,
and walking fast down the road, with the crunch of my
shoes loud, I felt I was safe. The streetlights left no darkness on this long stretch, and I was completely alone. I
waved down an auto-rickshaw, and was at the station
three turns and five minutes later.

I paid, and was almost at the ticket window when

a man leaning against the iron fence raised his chin in inquiry: what do you want? I looked a moment too long, but kept moving, and now the man was walking beside me, with that cheery, insinuating tout's whisper: "What you looking for, boss? You want some fun, haan? Charas, Calmpose, everything I got. You want a woman? Look at that auto there. All ready for you."

There was an auto parked across the road, pulled in deep at an angle in front of a shuttered shop. The driver was leaning on it, and I saw the glow of his bidi, and knew that the man was looking straight at me. The bidi moved, and the driver motioned against the back window of the auto, knocking, and a figure moved inside it, and a woman's head leaned out on the left side, into the lamplight. All I could see of her was the black shine of her hair, and the strong yellow of her sari, but I didn't need to see any more to know what sort of raddled randi sold her chut at stations in the back of an auto. I laughed, and paid for my ticket.

But the pimp stayed with me. "Okay, boss," he whispered chummily on the way to the platform gate. "I misjudged you, saab. You want something better. You're a man of fine tastes, my mistake. You just look a little, you know . . . But I have the girl for you, boss." He kissed his fingers. "Her husband used to work in a bank, was a big saab, poor fellow, then he had an accident. Complete cripple he became. Can't work. So she has to make a living for both of them, what to do? Very exclusive. Only for some gentlemen, you see, in her own apartment. I can take you straight there. You'll see what a high-class cheez she is, boss. Completely convent-educated."

I stopped. "Is she fair?"

"Like Hema Malini, bhidu. You touch her skin and you'll get a current. Like fresh malai."

"How much?"

"Five thousand."

"I'm not a tourist. One thousand."

"Two thousand. Don't say anything. You see the girl, and if you think she's not worth the money, you give me whatever you want and I'll leave quietly and not a word more. Believe me, if you saw her outside her husband's bank you wouldn't believe she has to do this, poor woman. Like one phataak memsaab she looks."

"What's your name?"

"Raja."

I put the train ticket in my back pocket. "All right, Raja," I said. "Just don't make me angry."

Raja giggled. "No, saab, no. Please come."

She was fair, no question. She opened the door and even in the bleary light from the lift I saw that she was fair, not quite Hema Malini-pale but light like afternoon wheat. She sat on a brown sofa while Raja counted his two thousand and bowed himself out. She wore a dull green sari with gold borders, and round gold earrings, and sat very respectable and contained with her shoulders high and hands in lap.

"What's your name?" I said.

"Seema," she said, not meeting my stare.

"Seema." I shifted from one foot to the other by the door, not sure of what to do next. I was experienced all right, but in a different kind of establishment, and the shiny glass table with its vase of flowers and the painting on the wall with just colours dashed together and the short brown carpet, all of these stopped me altogether. But she stood and went further into the apartment, and I stepped up manfully, taking it all in, the stretch of her blouse across the sunken river of her spine and the white phone in its alcove in the wall of the passageway. She clicked on a lamp in the bedroom, and when she flipped back the bedcover I tensed: it was altogether too professional. I had seen the same folding down of the sheets before, the same towel.

"Hold on," I said, and went back out into the hallway. The bathroom was clean, and I pissed into the western-style commode with some satisfaction, at length. But then I saw that there was no soap near the tap, no bucket. I zipped. The cupboards in the kitchen were empty, not a plate, not a pot, not even a gas or a stove, only two glasses drying upside down next to the basin. Now I was sure that I had been fooled. The apartment was nobody's home, not a bank saab's, not a good wife's, there was no cripple and no memsaab, only a whore got up and powdered. She lay on the bed, naked but for the earrings, her arms crossed over her small breasts and her belly rising and falling under the thin shadow of her hipbone, and one ankle over another. I stood over her, breathing through my mouth.

"Speak English," I said.

"What?"

In her eyes there was real surprise, and I grew more angry. "I told you. Speak English."

She had a sharp little nose and a small retreating chin, and she was puzzled for another moment, and then she laughed, just a very little bit and bitterly amused. "Shall

I speak?" she said. Then she spoke in English, and the words rattled around my head, and I knew that they were really English, I felt it in the crack of the consonants. "Bas?" she said.

"No," I said. I was hard, vibrating deep at the root. "Don't stop." She spoke English while I took off my clothes. I turned around to take off my pants and hide the revolver from her. When I turned back she was staring at the ceiling and speaking English. I nudged her ankles apart. "Don't stop," I said. I ground and bucked on top of her and she turned her face to the side and spoke. I reared up and the skin on her neck was sandy under the lamplight and I could hear her words. I understood none of it but the sound of it was an angry excitement inside my head. Then I felt a distant overflow, far below, and I was still.

I was very tired, Sardarji. I leaned forward into my walk. I was going back to my gold. The momentum of nearly falling over at every step kept me moving, but at every exhausted buckling of my knees I grew more afraid. I was very close to the gold now, I recognized every intersection and the shapes of particular buildings and shadowed trees. There was no moon but it was a light night, and out in this unbuilt open ground I saw clearly the black direction of the road and the white of a milestone. The gold was gone, taken, I felt a hole in my chest. It was gone, vanished out of my life. I should give up now. It would be easy for me to find a patch of grass by the road, tip over into it, sleep. Stop it. Ganesh Gaitonde, keep going. You have won every game today. Win again. You know exactly where you are.

The calculation of the precise section of barbed-wire fence was not a problem. I counted off the posts, looked up and down the way, and rolled under. Under the trees I passed into disastrous black, and was lost. With one hand extended I went gliding, rustling through space, not sure of the distances now, but I felt and reached and at the right moment I stopped and turned to the right. A step, and there was the tree. I passed a hand down the trunk and the ground below was flat. All around the trunk I went, feeling with both hands. After two circles, maybe three, I leaned a shoulder against it and made a long bleating sound. Ganesh Gaitonde, Ganesh Gaitonde. I scrabbled to the next tree, stopped when I grazed my head on it. Around it, around it. And then the next one. My cry was high now, a constant shriek under the canopy and darkness. It went without rise or fall in a half-circle. Stopped abruptly, because I had both hands on a fatness. The swelling rose out of the earth and filled both my palms. I traced it softly, up to the tree and down to the bottom of the mound, making out its shape. I moaned and dug both hands into it. I went rooting furiously into it, and welcomed the pain in my fingers. The cloth came first, and then the heavenly, familiar shape of a rectangle. My shoulders shook and I moved my hand and it was all there. All and undisturbed and mine. Up to my forearms in earth, I let my head drop and gulped in the smell of grass and my armpits and my body and knew that the world was mine. As dawn came I wrapped myself around the mound and slept with my revolver under my breast.

Eye in the Sky

Anjum Hasan

JASIM SAYS THAT DAWN is making too much noise eating that watermelon, she is slurping and chomping and whistling faintly as she spits out seeds, while he tries to focus on taking a few good photographs of a bright orange garbage compactor on the street below which will drive off any minute now leaving the dull cement and asphalt colours, the dusty buses and faded people, the wasted February browns and greens of the view from their bal-

---

ANJUM HASAN (1972–) is the author of one of the best novels to have appeared recently in the world of Indian fiction, *Lunatic In My Head* (2007), set in the northeastern town of Shillong where she grew up. Hasan has also written a book of poems, *Street on the Hill*, and as this story shows, hers is a poet's prose, able without striving to fashion something strange and delicate from the familiar. In 2009 Hasan published an acclaimed sequel to *Lunatic* called *Neti, Neti*. She now lives in the southern metropolis of Bangalore, and perhaps it is from there that the protagonist in "Eye in the Sky" sets out on her journey to Goa.

---

cony, colours that cannot be photographed because they are dying. They have been married for three years and Dawn knows what to do—she must chomp harder and spit out the seeds with greater force so that instead of landing on a potted aster, her previous aim, they can go through the wrought iron whorls of the railing and float two floors down to land on the heads of people who are coming out of the elevators in the basement of the apartment block and heading towards their cars to take off for their Saturday evening out.

She will play at this exaggeration till Jasim cuffs her gently on the head and then she'll stop so that they can kiss. But Jasim doesn't; he is motionless behind his camera though the compactor is already moving away and the light is starting to fade.

Without looking at her, he says, "Please . . . you sound disgusting."

"You try eating a watermelon quietly."

"Go away."

She stands up, her sticky hands making her helpless, and says, "I'm going, you jerk."

Inside, she washes her hands, combs her hair, picks up her handbag, and bangs the front door hard as she goes out. In the elevator down she knows that by the time she is at the small supermarket, doing her weekend grocery shopping, the peeve will have evaporated, and she can already think ahead to the arrival of that everyday calm even though right now she hates Jasim and wishes she had been even noisier. But when she comes to the shop, out of which spill smug children clasping their bars of chocolate and bottles of soft drinks, she doesn't feel like going in.

She walks past it—this shop full of people who have not just had fights with their husbands or wives—although she has no intention of going anywhere else. She feels ridiculous but it is too late to turn back so she continues walking on the broken pavement, trying to convince herself that the fight is over. Jasim will have forgotten and now be inside, spooning tea leaves into a teapot with the same care that he does everything else. The street has only large, glass-fronted stores full of mannequins with plastic faces and human bodies, barbers, cellphone shops, vegetable vendors behind pushcarts; soon she is in a stretch with just apartments and their sluggish security guards, no longer even the odd shop from which she could buy something to justify this needless walk. She can hear Jasim in her head, telling her to go away, and thinking back to their previous fights, she realises that they are abandoned rather than resolved. A better instinct always takes over; they very quickly feel stupid and stop quarrelling about how one of them is finicky beyond reason about clean spoons or the other a poor listener.

When she is a good kilometre from home, Dawn starts to grow contemptuous of her better self. If she and Jasim actually followed their fights to the end, where would they take them? She comes to a junction from where the busy main road she is on continues with its dirty-smelling traffic into the distance, while the road cutting across it is smaller and quieter and littered with the yellow bell-shaped flowers of the only tree that comes to life every year in this desert weather. Dawn turns into this mysterious road, which she passes without really noticing on her way to work everyday. She speaks to an invisible and just arbiter, telling him or her—this is what Jasim said, he said—go away. She knows that if she strays too far she will be lost because she is easily lost and has no sense of direction whatsoever. But that's what Jasim told her—he said, get lost. She takes another turn onto a busier road and almost at once there is a small, fenced-in, grassy patch of a traffic island on the far side of which stand empty, gleaming white coaches with their rearview mirrors hanging like great, inverted ears on either sides of their square faces. A backlit board announces Mysore, Hampi, Sravanbelagola, Goa. . . . Dawn realises she is wrong—she has been here before. This is from where she and Jasim took the overnight coach to Goa last year; as she walks past the coach stand, the memories of sea and grilled prawns and sand in the folds of her shorts and an inordinate number of Bacardi Breezers come to her and she tries to test them for truthfulness.

The truth is that she and Jasim were happy then and are happy now and it is a regular Saturday—they have snapped at each other as they occasionally do but soon they will make up and have tea together after Dawn has put away her shopping. Jasim will show her what he thinks are the best pictures of the compactor and they will play chess afterwards or plan where to go for dinner. Everything will fall back into the ordinary rhythm of happiness which is sustained only by repetition. Why is it then that Dawn has walked on and turned another corner, noticing, as if some veil of dullness had lifted from the world, the small auto repair shops full of men the same colour as their greasy carburettors, a petrol pump, bakeries and gambling kiosks and, eventually, a new-looking slum for the workmen on the towering office building coming up opposite, a slum full of children whose games send them running helter-skelter into the traffic. When she reaches the end of the road she thinks of the tea gone cold and knows Jasim will realise now that she has been gone for too long and call her; at that very instant she feels the phone buzzing against her thigh and she pulls it out of the pocket of her jeans.

She answers him as if nothing were the matter.

"I'm coming. There was a huge crowd in the super-market."

As if embarrassed, they never refer to their arguments post-facto, so how can Dawn explain that she is stand-ing in the middle of an unknown street because she does not want to come back home and pretend that the fight is over? Jasim tells her he can come down and help to bring the stuff up if she wants and she says—no don't, there's not that much. Jasim never goes shopping—five minutes in a crowded shop can give him vertigo. Some-thing about trying to decide whether the discount on a two-litre carton of cooking oil is worthwhile, something about the smell of a hundred packs of washing powder stacked together, the fidgety boredom of people standing in a checkout queue depresses him so much he feels giddy. It doesn't matter, because Dawn can shop, but Jasim is always trying to make up for this shortcoming in small ways.

Dawn feels that if she were to take one more turn she will have unraveled her life completely and never be able to knit it back together again. Has the long walk exhausted her anger and is she ready to go home? She

turns around and gingerly takes the first step back as if
walking on ice. Soon she is returning the way she came
and it is already night and nothing is resolved. There is
still a pebble in her chest and she wants to take it out
and fling it back at Jasim, but she cannot think of a good
reason to. That is why, when she comes to the coach stand
again, she crosses the road, goes into the ticket office,
and, with a great lurch of fear and exhilaration, buys a
ticket for an overnight coach to Goa.

"The old Finnish man from number four was so tight the
other day, he left without paying and came back later and
he was so tight I could hardly understand what he was
saying but I think he was saying, 'I left my boots here,
where are they?' I said to him, 'You haven't paid for the
room,' and the old guy said, 'My friend will come and pay
later, where are my good leather boots?'"

Dawn knows she is not dreaming but she turns onto her
side nevertheless, expecting that this position will make
the voice go away. Then she sits up in shock as the guard's
voice continues, seemingly under her bed, but actually
outside the window. Though Maria, the hotel owner, is
questioning him about the old man without his boots, she
sounds resigned to the fact that he has cheated her, just
as Shankar, the guard, seems to know that this is nothing
but a mildly funny story because he has already moved
on from it and is now arguing with the other guard who
insists on his right to dream about America. "America's
shitting in its pants right now my friend, I'm telling you
life is hard there while here you can sit in the shade when
its sunny and drink coconut water and when the monsoon

comes you go back home and teach your children manners." The other guard shifts ground. "I was thinking of Italy actually. Where my cousin has a good life. He walks around all day chatting with the tourists. If he can sell a dozen roses a day, he's set."

Dawn goes back to sleep and when she finally gets up it's noon; she goes to the window and sees the dogs asleep in the pits they have dug themselves in the sand of the hotel grounds, three kingfishers perched on a withered bush which they immediately leave in a whirr of brilliant green, and in the distance a family of acrobats practicing their moves, playing their dholak while a tiny girl walks across a tightrope with the languid boredom of a cat. The guards and Maria are gone and there is only the old woman caretaker there now; she has one tooth, wears a printed yellow frock, and sits slumped in her plastic chair, listening to a tape recorder with earplugs.

Jasim cannot believe what Dawn has done and will not talk to her, will not answer his phone, will not acknowledge that he's the one who asked her to go away. When the coach was starting she called him, and at first he was only puzzled. He had already forgotten the few minutes of their argument; "Why Goa?" he kept asking as if there was a hidden logic here but there was none, and Dawn, finding that she could not convince him of the justness of her anger, was left with the lame excuse of whimsicality.

"I just felt like," she said. "I know it sounds bizarre but I just felt like."

"You're lying," said Jasim and Dawn imagined him picturing all kinds of absurd scenarios but he contradicted this by adding "You're downstairs and you're on your way up."

"Can't you hear the coach?" asked Dawn, feeling she had done something so unnecessary it was beginning to seem ugly. "I didn't want to go," she said, close to tears now. "Why can't you see? I wanted to come back home but . . ." A bold new thought struck her and the tears retreated. "I'm bored of how it always has to be perfect."

This was too much for Jasim; instead of losing his temper he announced in a quivering voice that he was hungry and going to cook. Dawn said she would call later but later he refused to answer and now she looks at her phone (which holds no messages or missed calls from Jasim) and thinks with both terror and satisfaction that this is their first real fight. All night in the coach, because she was travelling alone, she felt she was travelling with a stranger, and the disturbing oddness of this kept her from falling asleep. There were also the continuous shrieks from a group of high-spirited college boys who called each other fucker or dude or mister lover; the clamour of their night-long conversations from the rear of the bus had sometimes risen above the sound of the engine and reached Dawn in front. "The Bangalore chicks are too easy . . . Vinay, have you got your hand up my shirt . . . I'm telling you, no Indian can ever be a world-class swimmer . . . wake up fucker otherwise I'm going to fart."

But waking up in this low-ceilinged room in which the fan whirred soundlessly as she slept but now makes a racket, Dawn feels a little less shy of herself and less ashamed of her audacity. She likes the room's bareness— pale creamy walls with the single line of a curly blue wave painted halfway up, little scratched table, spotted mirror, cupboard without hangers—and the fact that this bareness is encroached upon by nothing but her handbag. If Maria had asked her about her luggage, Dawn had a story ready—the rickshaw driver in Bangalore had made off with it when she'd stopped at a pharmacy on her way to the coach stand. And if the combination of her being alone and luggageless provoked curiosity, Dawn had a story ready for that too.

She takes a shower; there are no towels so she stands under the fan with the curtains drawn across her window and feels the drops evaporating slowly. Then she goes down to the beach where the parasailers are being strapped into their harnesses one after another, each taken up into the sky for five minutes, pulled by a motorboat whose every movement mirrors the parachute's arc across the sky and its curved descent. Coming down they always manage, incredibly, to miss the restaurant shacks and the sunbathers, and land more or less exactly from where they took off.

One of the restaurant waiters wants to give Dawn a massage but she nods him away. Because she is alone she drinks lime sodas instead of Bacardi Breezers and, leaning back on the cane chair, she tries to call to mind some image of what her life was like before she married Jasim.

Instead she finds herself listening without needing to eavesdrop on the conversation of a group of Englishmen and women at the next table.

A girl says, "We slept really well that night. We slept tight."

A man says, "There were people coming out with their eyes rolling or totally spaced out. One girl was crying."

Another man says, "He doesn't want donations. He doesn't want you to say anything. You just go in there and listen to him. That's all he wants."

The first man says authoritatively, "He is crucified every Friday and resurrected every Monday."

Dawn expects the whole group to burst into laughter but they don't, they just go on eating their chips and their tandoori pomfret and naans with serious expressions.

Boys come up to Dawn and try to sell her DVDs; women want her to buy sarongs and fruit and cloth satchels. What was her life like then? In the burning peace of noon, the faraway roar and retreat of the waves, the clear-cut conversations around her, the ecstatic smell of garlic frying in butter, and the great blue and white globe of sand, sky, and sea in which all of this is sealed to prevent anything like unhappiness from leaking in, Dawn finds that the answer eludes her. She has always thought of herself as admirably normal and there has been nothing but normalcy in her life everywhere she looks. She has never really wanted to be alone, examine her thoughts in private. It wouldn't have been normal. So she was never alone and then she married Jasim and stayed that way.

The waiter asks again if she wants a massage. It's very cheap. An elderly birdwatcher couple in khaki shorts and caps, laden with binoculars and cameras, sits down to drink beer. Another birdwatcher stops by and asks them in very articulated German tones "So vot did you see this morning?" The elderly couple starts to explain. Their enthusiasm is incredible. They smile in amazement at the memory of every rustling wingtip and birdcall.

An Indian man in trousers too thick for the beach and heavy shoes stomps on the beach shouting into his cellphone. "I still haven't got the cheque and I have to pay my bill. I came here thinking you'll be here but you weren't. Why can't you just give me the money? Yesterday your wife called me a beggar and I took all that calmly, but now I can't wait any more. I just can't . . . OK. Should I wait here? OK."

So why is Dawn here alone, inviting the stare of the Indian man as he walks away slowly?

Maybe she has suddenly become the woman in the song, the one who at the age of thirty-seven realised she'd never ride through Paris in a sports car with the warm wind in her hair, the one who at the end of the song goes to the rooftop and bows a curtsy to the night. Dawn watches the sea steadily, ignoring the staring man, and thinks, I can't want to kill myself because I'm hungry and it's not possible to feel both things at once.

"Massage madam?" asks the waiter, and he is not hopeful now, just arrogant in the way he stands squarely before her. When she doesn't move her eyes from the horizon, he takes her empty glass away. Then he hears someone calling his name, puts the glass back before Dawn, and falls into the arms of a large foreign woman whose skin has cooked and peeled and cooked and peeled so many times over it is like the underside of a fried egg— white patches showing through the pink-brown. They kiss each other on the mouth. Dawn is looking at them but no one else does. There is nothing incongruous in Goa about a

stick-thin waiter-masseur boy (whose English has, over
its rough Indian accent, the patina of something singsong
and charming and foreign) kissing a woman with whom
he obviously has nothing in common whatsoever.

In the late afternoon Dawn goes and buys a white cotton dress, changes into it in the bathroom of a café, then
sits down to order something to drink. Behind her she
hears a family chatting with a lone man at the table next
to them. They don't know each other well but neither is
this their first conversation. After a few hours in Goa,
Dawn remembers this— how tourists despite being tourists quickly settle into grooves, how they exchange familiar greetings with the Kashmiri salesmen who lounge
outside their shops full of things too rich for this weather
(hand-embroidered rugs, enormous emerald and tur-
quoise pendants embedded in white boxes, heavy bronze
sculptures); how they ride bicycles in pairs into the heat,
calling to each other; how they lean forward to talk to
strangers across tables. Dawn feels prickly and alone, so
alone that even Jasim's being here, assuming an entirely
different set of circumstances, wouldn't have been of help.

"I hate siestas," says the lone man who is a Canadian
landscape architect. "My grandmother used to force me
to take them and I would always wake up grumpy."

He starts to talk about his fifteen-year-old son studying in a school so fancy they row out to Lake Ontario and
have geography lessons on a boat. The Swiss couple has
two teenage daughters who sit there saying nothing, and
the Canadian says, with reference to them, "I should have
brought my son. I don't know . . . he's a handsome boy."

They all laugh. Then they start to talk about airfares.

The woman says, "It's the skiing break right now in Switzerland. I love the snow and yet I can't stand the winters."

The Canadian has been coming to Goa every winter for the last five years. Always alone. He sounds so relaxed and content, Dawn is compelled to steal a glance at him. He looks normal. Big red face and red Hawaiian shirt.

She orders another drink and no one looks at her and slowly the prickliness goes. There is no eye in the sky in Goa and here she can take her revenge on Jasim simply by not missing him. Then for the first time the thought strikes her that he might take his own revenge for this revenge. His silence is not his response to what she has done. His silence is merely a preparation for his response. And what will that be? Dawn tries to imagine the horror of going back and finding the house empty. She will make toast and forget to wipe the counter clean of crumbs. She will take down all the photographs pinned up on the board— Jasim's best pictures, selected after endless scrutiny and debate. She will unbecome the part of her that is Jasim.

His extreme sensitivity was puzzling to her in the early days of their marriage. He hated noise, demanded routine, loved things to be in rows and shiny spotless. He would stand in the kitchen and suffer when Dawn did the laundry because she always forgot to separate the dark colours from the light, or didn't use enough detergent. He was tortured by the children who rode their tricycles loudly in the apartment's corridors because of their dangerous unpredictability. Slowly, Jasim became a bit of Dawn and stopped opening the door and threatening the children every evening. And Dawn became a lot of Jasim

and got used to straightening and cleaning and refining
everything.

When the air cools a little and Dawn is making her
way down the village road back to the beach, a boy starts
to walk alongside her.

"Hello, hello."

It is one of the noisy boys from the coach, separated
from his companions. She nods at him.

"You're alone and I'm alone so I thought we could talk."

"I'm not alone. There's a husband," she says and grins
as if she has caught him out.

The boy extends his hand and Dawn shakes it. "My
name is Vinay. How much fun is it to be alone in Goa?
My friends have gone to Blue Fox to dance all night, but
I like to watch the sunset and talk."

His lines are rehearsed. Has he been following her?

They are nearing the entrance to her hotel; she turns
swiftly and walks into it. She knows he is coming behind
her, ruffling the sand softly with his floaters.

The guards are still discussing America. Shankar says,
"Your balls will turn to ice cream in the cold and you'll
use up all your savings making weekly phone calls to your
family. Here things are OK—you can live on rice and dal
and you have climate change."

Dawn realises he means that here we have changing
climates.

On the porch next to hers, she can hear a couple talking in rapid French, loud enough to suggest that they
know no one will understand them. She sits down on the
stained chair of her own porch and Vinay stands at some
distance, staring at her as if she was made of stone.

The guard comes over to her and says, "Good you chose this beach. The next one is rubbish."

"Who is this boy?" she asks, pointing to Vinay.

The guard doesn't know but is unconcerned. He seems not to take his duties as a guard too seriously.

"Do you want to take a taxi into the town tomorrow?" he asks.

Something is loosening in Dawn. Perhaps it is because nothing is a problem in Goa. She does not want a taxi into town, and yet the guard has gone off to get her a coconut full of water—it's one of the four he brought down this morning and the water is sweet he tells her, as he brings back the coconut and hacks at it clumsily with a small knife. He would like her to try it. She sits there sipping water from the gash Shankar has made. Vinay comes closer and says, "Your dress is sexy."

"Why didn't you go out with your friends?"

"I saw you and you looked like you were dying to talk."

Dawn sees that there is a music here into which everything flows—Vinay's cool stare, the lazy talk of the guards, the friendly calls of the Tibetan women selling silver bangles and knitted socks, the Kashmiri men, the Malayali Ayurvedic experts, the boys on the beach who will take you up into the sky for five hundred rupees, the waiters who come and sit on the restaurant chairs in between lunch and dinner, when there are only scattered beer-drinkers left, the cheerful signs everywhere—Full Moon Party Tonight, Group Tours to Anjuna Flea Market From Here, Five Free Kings Beers with a Whole Tandoori Chicken. Perhaps it is the waves which make

the music the sea which she can hear from here and
see a tiny fringe of through the palm trees. The sun has
vanished and she wants to be on the beach one last time,
be herself without Jasim, without their fight, without her
history. Alone in a white dress without thoughts.

She gives the empty shell of the coconut back to the
guard and walks away. Vinay catches up with her and
says, "Hello Goa friend" as if they've just met. He puts
out his hand again and this time when Dawn takes it, he
doesn't let go. Soon his fingers are intertwined with hers.

They go to the restaurant where she had lunch. Something to drink. A view to look—of sandcastles left by
fathers and their toddler sons, a sun which has blotted
out in the sky rather than tipped over the horizon, and
dogs going away, woken from their day-long naps by the
evening breeze and looking now for a different bed for the
night. The restaurant is filling up with people who will
spend a very long time deciding what to eat for dinner—
they invent amusements like that to fill the time with.

Vinay says, "I just love this frigging place. Come here
every year and never stop loving it."

An Englishman with enormous sideburns and round
glasses appears with a banjo and what was the rear of the
restaurant when the sea was visible, now becomes the
front. He sits on a high stool and sings old jazz numbers.
Dawn feels herself part of the murmur of the talk and the
tinkle of music.

"I thought you were a foreigner till you took off your
sunglasses just now at the hotel," says Vinay. He is sitting
close to her.

Dawn cannot think of what to say to this.

"You know how it is—you see a foreign chick and want to chat her up a bit because usually she doesn't mind. In fact, if she's alone she doesn't mind at all. But an Indian girl? I never trouble Indian girls. You're the first."

"So why are you troubling me?" asks Dawn. He moves closer to her.

"Because you lied about having a husband." As if absentmindedly, he puts his hand on her thigh. "You can't be married."

His hand is moving up and down now and Dawn suddenly wants to scream. She smiles and says brightly, "Suppose I ask the waiters to throw you out?"

Vinay smiles back and says, "You? A girl alone in Goa in a dress like that, making up stories about having a husband? You think they'll take you seriously?"

Two men come into the restaurant and sit down together. One of them was earlier shouting into his cell phone on the beach.

"Will you leave?"

"No," says Vinay coolly. "Come on baby. I just want to buy you a beer. And then I'll walk you to your hotel. I'm staying next door."

The musician's smoky jazz tunes sound all wrong to Dawn now. They belong to a world in which there are no worries, only heartbreak.

Dawn pushes his hand away and stands up.

"I'll tell them you've run away from Bombay or somewhere," says Vinay and sips his drink. "I'm sure you're up to something."

So he didn't see her in the coach last night. He will not

follow her back to Bangalore. She should just run to her room and lock herself in.

Instead she walks across to the two men and quickly sits down at their table. They look at her in amazement.

"Sorry," she says. "That boy is bothering me and I just wanted to get rid of him."

They turn to look at Vinay who has turned his back to them.

"No problem," says the cell phone man.

"I'll leave as soon as he goes. I'm just afraid he'll follow me if I go back to the hotel now."

The men ignore Vinay and offer Dawn a drink. They are celebrating the fact that after falling out with each other earlier in the week (because the wife of one called the other a beggar) they are now friends again. One of them—Johncy from Margao—is the author of several books including *Marry in Goa* which has recently gone into a fourth edition. The other—Patel from Pune—is a supplier of customised leather handbags and shoes to boutiques in Goa. They had fallen out over a money matter and now blame Johncy's wife whose tongue is too quick for her own good.

"I told her—you stay at home and think about your behavior," says Johncy. "Okay I've been pissed with Patel because for weeks he's been harassing me about that loan I took from him. But did I ever call him a beggar? Did I ever use that word?"

Patel looks sanctimonious. "She's a good-hearted lady. Sometimes she talks before she thinks, that's all."

"She's not upset that you left her at home and came here with Patel?" asks Dawn. She looks over Patel's shoulder at Vinay who is still waiting there, his back turned stiffly to her.

"No-oh," says Johncy. "She knows I need to go and have a drink now and then with my friends. What is life if you can't sit on the beach sometimes, eat some calamari, drink a few beers, talk to pretty ladies . . ." Here he winks at Patel, but Dawn is not offended.

"Just like you, no," says Patel. "You came here why?"

Dawn tells them how she came to be in Goa.

"I'm scared because Jasim's not answering the phone. I'm scared of what he'll do when I go back."

Patel clicks his tongue. "Nothing he will do. He'll be happy you came back."

Johncy is studying the menu and declares, "I'm going to eat a big red snapper today. Why? Because I feel like it."

The two men laugh and Dawn joins them, laughing heartily, loud enough for Vinay to hear. She realises that this is what she told Jasim last night. I'm going to Goa because I feel like it.

"My husband can't believe that I would come all the way to Goa. Just because we had an argument."

"Buy him a gift. Buy him some nice Goan feni. Two, three shots, he'll feel like forgiving the whole world," says Johncy.

"He doesn't drink," says Dawn and the men laugh uproariously again. There seems to be a lot that they find funny and when Dawn laughs with them she feels something lifting in her.

She sees Vinay getting up slowly and walking out of the restaurant without looking back.

Relief makes her say "But I'm so happy I came."

"Correct," says Patel in a pedagogical tone. "Once in a while, we must all run away. It's normal. Would you like a gin and tonic?"

I'm not a freak then, thinks Dawn. To have got onto that coach.

Patel takes her hand, studies her palm, then clicks his tongue rapidly. "Excellent, only excellent things here."

"Palmist, palmist," chants Johney, pointing at Patel. Then he signals to a waiter and asks to see the platter with the day's catch so that he can inspect his snapper before eating it.

Dots and Lines

Jayant Kaikini

WHEN CHANDRAKANT HABBU, who was from the banks of the Gangavali near Gokarn in Uttara Kannada district, and Deepotsav Mukherjee, from the banks of the Ganga in Bengal, met on Platform 2 in Miraj Junction, both were eating vade from the same stall. When Chandrakant had finished and was debating whether he should have another plate, Deepotsav, with his mouth full, seemed to say to him with his eyes, "Eat, man, eat . . . why are you hesitating?" Chandrakant had picked up the

JAYANT KAIKINI (1955–) is a short-story writer and poet. He was born in the temple town of Gokarna in Karnataka, which is where the protagonist of this story also comes from, and lived for many years in Mumbai before moving to Bangalore. This story describes the uncertainties of a youth leaving home for the first time, and it also beautifully illustrates the serendipities of train travel in India and the short, intense encounters with strangers that it spawns. As Kaikini shows, home sometimes looms largest in the imagination precisely when one is escaping from it.

courage to order another plate. After that, a kind of smiling relationship was established between them, and by the time the Mumbai-bound Sahyadri Express departed, they had strung their conversation on the tattered rope of broken Hindi.

Chandrakant's Hindi was derived from the Vividh Bharati radio cricket commentary—*Achchi gend, middle aur off stump ke oopar*—and from Hindi action films which would be shown in the cinema halls of Gokarn and Ankola. Deepotsav, on the other hand, would add "o" to every word and say "homko tomko," for "humko tumko." Chandrakant was reminded of the Konkani he would hear in his hometown. He had heard that these Bengalis, like the Konkanis, ate enormous quantities of fish. This constant "o" sound must be the effect of the fish. Deepotsav was returning from a football camp that was held somewhere in Kerala, while Chandrakant was taking the old man Beeranna Nayak from his neighborhood for a checkup at the Tata Hospital in Mumbai. Earlier, Beeranna Nayak had been taken there by his own son, and had come back after a prolonged medical treatment. He had been asked to return for a checkup after six months. Getting leave was difficult for his son, who was a teacher in a single-teacher school in a village near Yallapur. Even if he did manage to get leave, it would be leave without pay. So he had asked Chandrakant, who was anyway flying kites or playing volleyball for the youth club or swimming in the Gangavali, to accompany his father. Chandrakant's father, who worked in a flour mill, hesitated a bit, but Chandrakant did not want to let go an opportunity to see Mumbai at someone else's expense. They were to stay in the house of some relative. At the most, he would have to spend two whole days in the hospital. After that, one could watch a couple of films, see the glamour and glitter of Mumbai and have a good time, he thought and readily agreed to go.

Though initially he was not particularly perturbed about his trip to Mumbai, as the day for departure approached, he began to experience a strange fear, like someone about to appear for an examination. He took with him the kabaddi team T-shirt he had been given when he was in PUC, a couple of shirts and pants, and a pair of jeans borrowed from Pradeep who lived upstairs. He asked Aziz to lend him his smart Dubai shoulder bag. He held Beeranna Nayak's hand and helped him board the bus which brought them to Hubli.

In Hubli, despite Beeranna's protests, he made him walk around looking for a grand non-vegetarian hotel where they ate lunch. Though Beeranna, who was quite exhausted, asked for a rickshaw, he said no because the station was nearby. When he learnt that there were still two or three hours for the train to arrive, he left Beeranna at the station and went out, telling him that he would be back soon. He then took a rickshaw, went to a cinema theatre, and watched a film sitting on the edge of his seat. Just as the fight sequence at the climax of the film started, he scrambled out, and since he could not get a rickshaw, he ran all the way to the station.

Beeranna, who trusted him completely, was waiting for him, not even remotely anxious. Chandrakant's heart was pounding as he struggled to get Beeranna Nayak and their two bags into their train. Just then Deepotsav had come from inside and helped Beeranna up. "I shall find a seat for him. You get the luggage," he had said. As soon as he found a seat, Beeranna went off to sleep, unconcerned about food and water.

Chandrakant's heart was still beating fast. The thought that they might have missed the train if he had been five minutes late frightened him. The whole train appeared inhuman to him. Women squabbling over seats in loud voices, men sitting opposite them like statues with no expression on their faces.

Just as he was recovering from the hustle and bustle of his first train journey, someone came in saying, "meals, meals." Chandrakant bought two plates. He shook the old man awake, and giving him a plate, said, "Beerannajja, eat your food." Woken up from deep sleep, a bewildered Beeranna ate in a hurry, completely oblivious of where he was, and spilt rice all over himself. When he wanted to wash his hands, Chandrakant sounded somewhat irritated. "There's a big crowd over there. Wash your hands here at the window," he said, sprinkling some bottled water on his hands. He was most agitated that the others in the compartment might find out that he was traveling by train for the first time.

After a while Ghataprabha station arrived. Everyone got good meals, which they relished. "Arre, this meal is better. Maybe I was in too much of a hurry," he thought. He felt upset again because everyone except him seemed to know about it. If Nayak asked him sleepily to close the window, or asked him, in a feeble voice, for biscuits or water, he would attend to him in a bad-tempered way, as if he was disgusted.

But in the presence of Deepotsav Mukherjee, Chandrakant got some confidence and felt calmer. It was Deepotsav who had helped Nayak get on to the train, and persuaded Chandrakant into eating vade. In Miraj, Nayak had said, "I want to urinate. Shall I do it here itself at the edge of the platform?" Even before Chandrakant could mumble, no, no, not here, Deepotsav told him, "Ajja, don't worry. It is better to do it out here than in the compartment. Come to this side, it is a little dark here." He had led Nayak by the hand, to one side, made him urinate, and helped him climb back into the compartment.

He was a young man more or less the same age as Chandrakant, with a sprouting moustache and a radiant fair face. Chandrakant felt very much at ease when Deepotsav came into the same compartment. His anxious moments melted away as Deepotsav effortlessly started a conversation. The train left Miraj at 9 o'clock in the night. Deepotsav kept his baggage on the berth above the window, a little distance away from Chandrakant's seat, and started taking out his toothpaste and brush. He was wearing a yellow windcheater and simple cotton shorts. As he went towards the washbasin, he smiled at Chandrakant and Beeranna Nayak and waved his hand as if to enquire whether they had found comfortable seats. Though he had soft canvas shoes on his feet, he would take them off and put them on within seconds. As soon as he saw the boots on Chandrakant's feet, weighing a ton and resembling the iron-hard military boots, he said, "Just take them off. Relax." After he undid the knotted-up laces, and removed his shoes and pushed them away under the seat, Chandrakant's feet felt lighter, and he found the touch of the train floor refreshing. Deepotsav, who saw Chandrakant staring at him, offered him toothpaste by stretching his arm forward. Not knowing what to say, Chandrakant told him he had some in his bag.

Deepotsav leaned against his bag in the upper berth and started reading a pink English book. Looks like a handsome hero, the lucky bastard. There must be a troupe of girls behind him, thought Chandrakant. Deepotsav patted the berth and beckoned Chandrakant to come up. Though he wanted to go, Chandrakant somehow felt shy and shook his head. "Call me Deepu, as my football teammates call me. What shall I call you?" Chandrakant didn't know what to say. He just smiled. "Why friend? What does your girlfriend call you?" Chandrakant got even more perturbed and said nothing. Deepu left him at that and started reading.

Chandrakant's mind went around his world in Gangavali-Gokarn. He got absorbed in deep thought trying to figure out who his girl was. Was it she who had left her softness in his hands forever, who had giggled, saying it tickled her, when he had held her for a few moments beside the shed in the neighboring alley on the night of the Yakshagana peformance? Was it the Maths teacher's daughter, who had been staring at him endlessly, right from the fourth standard to the eighth, pulling down her blouse all the while? Was it the beauty who waved to him as she left, to thank him for taking her handbag and reserving a seat for her before she got into the bus? Who . . . who? Who was his girl? Chandrakant couldn't think of anyone.

Again, Deepu patted his thigh gently. "Why my friend?

What are you worried about? All the girls in your mind are yours. They come to your mind whenever you call them. They are all yours. All the things that you like in the world are yours. Where else can they stay so warm and secure as in your mind?" he said. "Look at him! How easily he lifted the burden off my heart!" thought Chandrakant, and smiled sheepishly.

All the people in the compartment had spread their blankets and beddings on their seats and were preparing to go to bed. Chandrakant had only a lungi in his bag. People were switching off the lights. A fat woman nearby pulled a gown over her head and in a flash pulled off her sari from underneath. Then she smeared some oil-like cream on her face and started folding her sari. Chandrakant was staring at her in wonderment when Deepu whispered in his ears, "She too is yours!" and laughed.

"Put grandfather to bed," he said later. "I should, of course," thought Chandrakant and returned to his seat. Then his heart missed a beat. Beeranna Nayak was not in his place! People on either side were preparing to go to bed. As he was wondering where the old man could have disappeared, Nayak came from the toilet walking rather unsteadily, and sat down, out of breath. Chandrakant tried to show a little anger and asked him why he didn't call him for help. But there wasn't sufficient annoyance in his voice. "You may go now," said Nayak.

Chandrakant went towards the toilet. It looked as if someone was inside. He stood outside, swaying. The train was chugging along in the dark. He was distressed as he wondered why he felt so helpless when Beeranna Nayak disappeared for a moment. Why did he feel so much braver in Nayak's presence? He felt he had been waiting for too long and pushed open the door. There was no one in the toilet. Chandrakant came out realizing that urinating in a moving train was as tricky as throwing rings around the targets in the stalls of Bandihabba fair.

The lights went out one by one and Beerannajja was struggling to untie the knot in his bag. Chandrakant helped him, and Beerannajja took out two blankets and a bedspread and offered one to Chandru. He made his bed with shaking hands. Taking out Amrutanjan from his bag, he rubbed it on his forehead, knees, and hands. "Chandru, we reach Pune around midnight and Mumbai early in the morning. It will get cold near Pune. Wear another shirt if you want," he said. He drank some water from the bottle. "Fill it up in some station or the other. Don't get off alone. Go down with that friend of yours." He fell asleep almost instantly.

Chandrakant crouched on the seat next to him. Deepu was sitting some distance away reading a book, with a Walkman in his ear. He looked so relaxed as he read, eating an orange someone had given him. Chandru decided to wait quietly till he finished eating.

At a distance, Deepotsav with the Walkman, looking like a dream. Here nearby, the sleeping Beerannajja, looking like the Gangavali in Gokarn. In between, the Sahyadri Express wobbling as it sped along. There was so much to see in Mumbai. Would the city absorb him as well? The train had already acquired a new look because of the behavior and clothes of the people who had got in at Miraj. A bus in Hubli or Belgaum or Gokarn did not look like this. There, the bags would be half-open. Stalks of vegetables and greens sticking out, a child's cap and stainless steel containers could be seen inside the bags. Or a flowered sari folded up and pushed in at the last minute.

Here were bags all properly closed, luggage with addresses neatly written and pasted on, and everything was as if ironed. A shining two-cell torch peeped out from Beerannajja's bag and watched everything. Chandru did not want to think of the banian and the two sets of clothes he had stuffed into his bag. Why wasn't he blessed with Deepotsav's good fortune of being able to wander around the country without hesitation and the ability to keep himself in tiptop condition?

A girl who was lying down under a blanket on the upper berth called out to Chandru from above and asked him if he could please switch off the light. "Oh, fine!" he said and switched off the light, then moved towards Deepotsav. "Can't you sleep, Chandru? Go there and stand by the door. Let us get some air. There is just a page and a half left. I'll finish the chapter and come," said Deepu.

Chandru went and stood by the door. How come Deepu had addressed him so familiarly as Chandru? Like his friends in the town used to. Like Thimmakka who lived next door, or like his own father—the same voice, the same way of speaking. How did a tongue from Calcutta catch the sound of Gangavali so exactly?

The door was shut tight. He raised the window. The sharp wind outside blew in, along with the chugging sound of the train wheels. Chandru felt happy about his small piece of good luck. How he had managed to get a trip to Mumbai without having to spend a paisa. How he was getting to see the world outside! If he were at home, he would be going from door to door collecting money for the Ganapati festival organized by the Youth Club in the village. As always, there would be quarrels—about banana stem decorations, about the swimming competition. How wonderful that this train journey had come his way!

The sound of the train was exactly like the sound of the flour mill where his father worked. All he had to do was close his eyes, and it seemed to him as if he was standing in his father's place collecting the flour. All day long his father would stand by the mill, feeding the grain and collecting the flour in a bin. With his whole body covered in flour, he looked like a flour ghost. In the evening, he would hone the millstones that would have become blunt.

Till the last minute, he had not been in favor of Chandru's journey. He had been a little worried. His son had taken someone else's money. What if he misused it? Or if something happened to old Beerannajja through the boy's negligence? He was worried about all that, but had given in when his wife said that it would be much better for the boy to see the outside world for a while instead of wasting time swimming in the swollen Gangavali during the monsoon, or chatting uselessly with good-for-nothing friends at Prabhu's shop, or staying awake all night in the company of bus drivers who had night halts in the town. So he had told Beeranna Nayak, "The boy is going out for the first time. You have been there before. Please look after him yourself." He had on his own given his son two hundred rupees as spending money.

Driver Gaju, who went at least twice a month on the

Mumbai line, from the Karwar Depot, had given Chandru quite a lot of information about Mumbai. How in a city, a human being becomes an ant, how time is money, and so on. He had gone on and on in that vein and had finally said that no one bothered about anyone here. Chandru had probably latched on to that one sentence. Because he believed that in the Gangavali, Bankikodla, and Gokarn region there were far too many people interested in other people's business. Everyone knew everyone else. You met the same people on the street. Though everyone knew everything about everyone else, they would still talk as if they knew nothing and offer advice as if they knew everything. They knew where and when the vegetables and fish arrived, who bought vegetables and fish worth how much, who walks away after much haggling, and who, unable to buy anything themselves, would persuade others, saying, "The fish is good. Buy it," and then feel happy as if they had made the purchase themselves. They knew which houses got newspapers from the afternoon bus, how Prabhu saved the daily paper in his teashop from people who read it for free, and then used it to wrap bhajis in.

And they also knew why Parameshwari, who had got married and gone to live in the hills last year, came home for Bandihabba this year and did not go back. She stayed on and opened a sewing class. It wasn't just one issue or two. Everything that was within and outside the world was shared equally by everyone else, like the pages of the newspaper, *Samyukta Karnataka,* from the teashop.

Hence, the small town was like a warm embrace for Chandru who had failed his PUC examination and stayed on in his hometown. It was an embrace in which he could

sleep at any time, any place. But the irritating habit of
people asking questions when they knew everything
annoyed him to no end. If his mother said, "They say
good fish has arrived, go and get some before others take
it away," he would reply, "Let it be. We had it yesterday.
Let the others enjoy it today." He was afraid of the teachers at school. He felt they were constantly reminding him
of all the things he couldn't do, and were warning him
that he was himself responsible for all his misery, his misfortune. So somehow he avoided any teacher. If he saw a
teacher on the street, he would sneak into a narrow lane,
jump into a field, or hide in some vegetable patch. After
giving it much thought, he had convinced himself that
it was the educated people who would build cities in the
future, or become eligible for the luxuries and ease of life
in the city. So, he would look at people from cities with
as much curiosity as envy. He would slink out of sight of
his classmates who had studied or worked elsewhere, or,
for that matter, of anyone who had come from the city.
He wouldn't meet them, but instead spend time in paddy
fields or by the river. He wouldn't even attend weddings.
The reason being that he was sure that there would be
respected citizens wearing pressed shirts who would ask
him, "Oh, you are his son, I see. What are you doing?"
Just like the questions a teacher would ask.

That was why driver Gaju who roamed around the
town, who had nothing in common with him, became
very close to him. Without his parents' knowledge, Chandru had, through Gaju, put in an application for a driver's
job in Karwar Depot. Just as he worried about whether
there was anything wrong with his wanting to become a

driver, he was also somewhat troubled by his desire to find pleasure in this Mumbai journey for which, as far as he was concerned, Beerannajja was only a pretext. Perhaps, that was why he lost his temper with Beerannajja over and over again. This journey, he thought, would hone his self the way the dulled surfaces of the grindstone were every day, and he was filled with both excitement and fear.

Deepotsav came down after closing his book and placed a hand on Chandru's shoulder. "Don't be scared. Open the door," he said, and pulled open the heavy door. A blast of cold air swept over both of them. Keeping his feet on the lower steps, Deepu sat at the door. Chandru sat right beside him, feeling scared. His legs were shaking. The train moved on, slicing through the night. Square patches of lights from the windows ran alongside the train. In the distance were twinkling lights of villages. A pale glow spread all around, as if to assure that the moon was nearby. Here and there, buses and lorries with open eyes were standing in a row at level-crossings, while the drivers smoked, leaning against the bonnets. Fields nodded their heads in the night wind. "How beautiful it is!" exclaimed Deepu. "Who knows when the drivers of the night vehicles sleep. Everyone in the train has drawn up their blankets and slept off. We don't even spare a thought for the engine driver who pulls us along safely on the tracks at night." Chandru thought it was absolutely true and felt thrilled.

A few minutes later Chandru said, "Deepu, I have decided to become a driver." It was as if his decision was made firm by giving expression to it. "Great, great," said Deepu.

After a while, Deepu started telling Chandru his story. His mother lived alone in a lovely village on the banks of the Ganga. There was a fishpond at the back of their house. They kept a variety of fish there. Whenever Deepu went home his mother would fry his favorite fish for him. Deepu had been running behind a football since his school days. He had wandered all over Bengal, chasing the ball. Because of his love for the game, he had begged and pleaded to be included either as a temporary member or as an extra in any small or big team in the city. He had run wherever the ball had called him. He would have bruised knees. He would eat just one meal a day. He went to various states as an extra for different teams. He had suffered the indignity of being dropped at the last moment, and spent days and nights in the waiting rooms of railway stations, holding fast to the dream that some day he would join Mohun Bagan, the famous football team of Kolkata.

He had obtained a diploma through correspondence and held a part-time job. At the moment, he was playing for a not-so-famous team in Kolkata. He would pay from his own pocket and participate in any camp that had excellent coaches. He was now returning from one such camp in Cochin. He liked scoring goals with a header. He would go to the village to see his mother once a month. He had never taken any money from her, he said. He had been interested in painting from a young age. He made greeting cards when he had time to spare. During the Navaratri Durga Puja festival, he sat up day and night making greeting cards. His mother made envelopes for him. He sold them through a friend's shop and made money. He would use the same money to attend training camps. He bought a Walkman with his earnings. If he found time, he would draw portraits of the players who were in the camp.

"The people who get their portraits done fall so much in love with them that they forget to pay," laughed Deepu. "Do you know how many great people, artists among them, ended up as beggars? Catch hold of any man who draws pictures on the pavement, writes slogans, and prepares posters. Give him soap and ask him to have a bath. Give him enough rice and fish to fill his stomach. Then give him paper and some colours. You will see a great artist emerging!" said Deepu, and fell silent in his anguish.

Tiny drops of rain came through the cool wind and fell on both of them sitting huddled together. "Ah!" they both exclaimed at the same moment.

"I like fried fish more than fish curry," said Deepu, while Chandru said that he liked crab and shellfish. "We tend to like whatever is cheaper. Isn't that so?" said Deepu and both laughed. "Of course, the joy you get from eating shellfish will not come from the most elaborate meal in the world. You are a lucky man. Our ladder to heaven is simple and small. Great. Great!" Deepu said. Deepu's favorite was Soumitra Chatterjee from Bengal and Chandru's was the Kannada actor Rajkumar. When Chandru asked who was good in Hindi films, Deepu talked in detail: "Jackie Shroff had a good athletic body. Aamir Khan was sweet and could easily be a jilebi hero. He wore high-heeled shoes in "Dil," in which he acted with Madhuri Dixit. Otherwise, how could he be of her height? If you think about it, you'll see that Kamal Hasan and Moon Moon Sen deserved better opportunities in Hindi films." He laughed loudly, then said, "Chief Minister Jyoti Basu's nose is excellent for a snuff advertisement." He told Chandru, "Don't see Hindi films. You must see English films. They are wonderful." "I see Yakshagana folk theatre. It takes place in a field all through the night. The dance, music, actors, the dialogue—everything is so wonderful that you are lost in it."

Meanwhile the train arrived at a deserted station. It made a pretence of stopping for a few seconds, when Deepu jumped down quickly, dragged Chandru to a cigarette stall, bought two cigarettes in a hurry, lit one, and lit the other one with it and gave it to Chandru. The train hooted. They ran and hopped on to the moving train. The activity, which took only a moment, sent a magical energy through Chandru.

"It has been years since I gave up cigarettes. I gave it up as soon as I started collecting money for football. Wills used to cost 25 paisa then. Now it has gone up to 60 paisa. The present weather, wind, night, and your company made me want to smoke. So I am smoking a cigarette Wah!" said Deepu, puffing happily.

Deepu, Gangavali, Kolkata, and the train—how did they all connect? How quickly they had run off and come back! Excited by all that, Chandru kept the cigarette in his hand for a long time. He hadn't smoked before. Not even when driver Gaju had tried to force him, not even when everybody was shouting and enjoying themselves after immersing Lord Ganapati in the water. The same Chandru sat watching the smoke clouds from Deepu's cigarette, and the one in his own hand wrapping a turban of ash around itself, warm and white, sparking red.

"Oh, no! Sorry, sorry! I didn't know you don't smoke. I am sorry I gave you a cigarette. Why didn't you tell me before?" said Deepu, taking the cigarette away from Chandru. "I shall offer it to the dear night," he said as he threw it away. It disappeared, showering sparks. As if encouraged by it, he threw away his cigarette as well. The two cigarettes, which burnt in the cool night and disappeared, made them feel as if they had warmed the place where they sat.

Then Deepu asked about Beerannajja. "Look, what you are doing is very good. Everyone looks for blood relations. Even people who have been neighbors for years in cities like Kolkata and Mumbai say that there is nothing they can do when someone dies. They believe that some relative or the other should come to take care and so call them up. So, what is the meaning of any relationship? Is it just for attending funeral rites?"

Then they both talked about their siblings. Chandru saw clearly for the first time the eyes, nose, and ears of his first cousin. He felt too twisted inside when he said that she stammered when speaking. "Don't worry," said Deepu, "It will go off by itself. Play with her at least for two hours. When you go swimming, take her along. Make her sit on the bank and talk to you. If love and attention is given to her, it will go off by itself. I have made a small peacock feather card. Give it to your sister. I shall give it to you later."

His sister was in Mumbai. She was married fifteen years ago. But the marriage broke up after five years. "Generally, Chandru, a girl comes back to her parents as soon as her marriage breaks up. But my sister—Jyotika is her name—she didn't come back. I feel proud of her. Neither did she wander around in society carrying her ledger of pain. She has taken up a room in a small colony and gives tuition to as many children as possible, applies mehendi to the palms of girls, and carries on with her life. For poor brides, she does this free. On the whole, she doesn't waste her time, instead, involves herself around. I see her when I go to Mumbai. She feeds me. But, as soon as it is time for work, she leaves. She doesn't utter a word about her tuitions. If I had been in her place, I would have bragged about it. But I found out all this from the neighbors."

Deepu said nothing for a short time. "We cultivate only those virtues that other people can see, isn't it? How many people are there who are good or do good deeds without others ever coming to know about it? That's why I like you. I was reminded of my sister Jyotika when I heard you were taking Beerannajja for a medical checkup."

The train was moving so fast, it seemed to be swaying in the wind. Just then the boy who went from compartment to compartment selling coffee reached them. They both drank some steaming coffee. "Forget all that. Let's talk about the happiest moments of our lives," said Deepu. Chandru just smiled dryly. Deepu continued, "Football players have no value in India. Only the cricket bastards are worth something. But you know, when in the drizzling rain, my partner gives a throw and I leap to the ball, dodging my opponents, dribble past my opponents cleverly, then direct it straight into the goal, the thrill is no less than Kapil Dev's when he scored that century against Zimbabwe."

Then Chandru narrated his experience. Two years ago he alone had taken the four-foot idol of Ganapati from the Youth Club's community Ganeshotsav, and swum far into the water where the river met the sea and immersed it there. When he looked back, he couldn't see the people, he could only see the shore. What a sense of triumph had surged through him. What an unforgettable moment it was! Even now he could feel his scalp tingle when he thought of it. He also recalled the thrill he had felt when he had cycled furiously to Gokarn in the middle of the night to fetch the doctor and get the medicines for the neighbor Thimmakka, whose condition had suddenly become serious.

Deepotsav got up. "Go and see your Beerannajja. He may want water to drink," he said. Chandru stumbled into the compartment. Deepu followed him. Beeranna did not look like he was asleep. His legs were shaking violently. "Beerannajja, do you want some water? Why are your legs trembling?" Chandru asked. "It's nothing," said Beerannajja and drank the water. "Because of weakness he must be exhausted. That's why his legs are trembling," said Deepu. He sat by Beerannajja and started patting and pressing his feet. Beerannajja closed his eyes, as if his discomfort was eased. "Let me do it, Deepu," said Chandru. "Why shouldn't I?" asked Deepu, without stopping what he was doing. Chandru could find no answer and sat staring at him. After a while, Deepu got up and went close to Beerannajja's face. Covering him with the blanket, he whispered in Chandru's ear, "He is asleep. You go and sleep now." Patting Chandru's back, he went up to his berth.

Deepotsav covered himself, put his head on his bag, and slept comfortably. There was a blue light in the carriage. Chandru couldn't sleep. Just a few hours ago, this Deepotsav was sitting far away listening to the Walkman, the Deepotsav who had sat by the open door and come close to him in the blowing wind, who had pressed Beerannajja's feet and gone up to sleep. . . .

By then, a station arrived. A chaiwalla was calling out, "Chai, chai." Chandru got up and went to the door. Everyone else had fallen asleep. He got down past the creaking door. It was an unknown station with unknown lights. Some people were getting in and out of the coaches. No one got down from his compartment. Not knowing how long the train would stop there, Chandru ran, bought himself some tea, got back in, and drank it standing up. The entire train and the whole platform were unfamiliar. There was a strange courage within him—the courage to rule the whole area around him.

Meanwhile, a woman with a water bottle was trying to wake her husband up, asking him to get some water. By the time Chandru got the bottle from her and filled it up, the train hooted. By the time he had put the lid on and started running back to the train, it had started moving. As he ran alongside the train, he could not recognize his compartment till he saw the woman put her hand out of the window, calling out, "*Paani, paani.*" He got confused about which door he should climb into. The train was gathering speed. Realizing he shouldn't waste another moment, he grabbed the bars outside the nearest door and hauled himself in.

Chandru, who had forgotten everything—his name,

the journey, and everything else for a moment—recollected it all as soon as he got in. The same train, but a different compartment. There wasn't much of a difference. He walked on looking this way and that across the shaking coach. Families asleep in the same way, a couple of villagers huddled near the door. Above and below in all berths, there were old men like Beeranna Nayak, asleep, wrapped up in a muffler, wearing a sweater, and smelling of Amrutanjan. And young men like Deepotsav and Chandrakant. Everyone was sleeping in the same manner, head on arms, and covered in a blanket. They were moving with the rhythm of the train in their sleep. Who among them were traveling for the first time, running away from home, or going to a hospital? Amidst all of them was a woman with a child sleeping next to her, feeling very uncomfortable on the narrow berth. Those who couldn't sleep sat with their heads on their knees, looking out of the window.

Chandru came to the door, opened it boldly, and sat down. It was the same wind, the night wind of a new locality. Deepu, whose voice had choked as he talked about his sister to a stranger like himself, was in the next carriage. His mother, who would take out his favorite fish from the pond and wait for him; Appa the flour ghost, who even now would take the best fish from his own plate to put it on Chandru's; Beeranna Nayak, who told him to wear an extra shirt as it would get cold in the night; Jyotikadidi, who would paint mehendi on the palms of poor brides as if it was a religious commitment on her part—they are all here in this very compartment. How well Deepu had put it—there is no safer, warmer, more secure place to live than in the heart. What would have happened if he had not been able to get back into the carriage? Nothing would have happened. Deepu would have gotten Beerannajja home safely.

Outside, the night was ripening. The plumes of the sugarcane plants were swaying in the starlight. In the harvested fields leaped the flames from the furnace of the sugarcane press. The people who sat in a small group around the fire looked like the laborers sitting around the fire warming their tabors on the night of Ganga's wedding and dancing and singing "chaboch" on the banks of the Gangavali. In a few moments the fire disappeared behind a hill. In the distance, the twinkling lights of a city appeared like stars that had secretly descended on to the earth. Maybe in another half-hour they would arrive at the city, or maybe they wouldn't.

Deepu had said when the switches of our pain and joy were right within us, why should we break our heads over the external geography?

A child could be heard crying: the same child. Carrying the child who wouldn't stop crying however much it was soothed, the mother came near the door. Chandru stepped back so that the wind could blow on them, but kept his arm across the door for safety. Thimmakka's daughter in Gangavali cried just like that all through the night.

"I came here because other people's sleep would be disturbed," said the mother, patting the child on the back and singing a lullaby in her own language. With the wind, the rhythmic swaying of the train, and the warmth of the mother's arms, the child became quiet gradually and fell asleep. For Chandru, the whole world seemed a very small and lovable place. The train was swaying and going downhill. The mother went in with the sleeping child. The distant city lights appeared like dots laid out for a rangoli design. Every dot was like a moment of fulfillment. Each person joins his own dots and gets his own design. Deepu, Chandru, Jyotika, Beerannajja, Kapil Dev—each one is busy completing his or her rangoli by connecting their dots. Chandru leaned outside the door and watched the swaying of the entire train. He could hear the coffee boy going from carriage to carriage. As soon as they reached a station, he must get coffee for Deepu and Beerannajja. The old man must be taken to the toilet and he must remember to collect the peacock feather card for his sister from Deepu.

Chandru felt that the wind that sang a lullaby and put the child to sleep had just blown the tarpaulin off the night-halting bus on the banks of the Gangavali before reaching this place. He stood watching the approaching rangoli of lights as if he was in charge of the whole train.

translated from Kannada by Padma Ramachandra Sharma

In the Moonlight

Lalithambika Antherjanam

"ANNAMME, did I hear you whispering? I won't have that, understand? I won't have you flirting with my son even before you've crossed the threshold of our house."

Annamma's mother-in-law peered out of the narrow, smoke-encrusted kitchen door, shaking her head hard in such disapproval that the long *kunukkus* in her ears rocked ominously. "It's dreadful. Young people are so shameless these days."

The stories of LALITHAMBIKA ANTHERJANAM (1909–1985) give voice to the struggles and anxieties of the women of her native Kerala. Antherjanam belonged to a caste group—the namboodiri brahmins—who prided themselves on their fidelity to tradition, which included a view of women as confined rigidly to the domestic sphere. (The word *antherjanam* literally means "one who lives inside.") Despite—or perhaps because of—these restrictions, Antherjanam managed to convey sympathetically the dilemmas of people both like and unlike her. This tender love story, which depicts a woman both metaphorically and literally incarcerated, is set among the Syrian Christian community and unfolds across two Christmases.

Anna called back from the courtyard where she sat oiling a pot, "I wasn't talking to anyone. I was just shooing away the crow that had overturned the pot."

"Now that's a lie if I ever heard one. I know Avuda is somewhere there. I saw him walk that way a minute ago. Avude!" she called out authoritatively. "What were you doing, working near the girl?"

"Nothing. I just happened to be walking by."

"There you are, I knew the girl was lying. Shooing away crows, indeed! I know what you're up to, my girl. Don't imagine that a chit like you can throw dust in my eyes! Listen to me, young fellow, what I have to say is meant for you too. If this sort of thing happens just once more, you'll have cause to remember!"

Avuda strode away without a word. There was so much he had to do, anyway. Anna turned and walked slowly to the well, crying, her eyes reddened. Lost in her thoughts, she threw in the palm spathe and swirled it as she bent over to draw the water. She had no eyes for the green spreading over the walls of the well, or for the water moving in its depths, although its eddying surface mirrored her own agitated heart.

They had been married almost six months now. Avuda was sixteen, Anna fifteen, but she was a whole foot taller than him. Young girls grow rapidly, and tire of growing just as fast.

Theirs was a household that adhered very rigidly to the Catholic custom of not allowing newlyweds to meet or to talk to each other. And Anna's mother-in-law seemed exceptionally clever at ensuring that this custom was strictly observed. Recalling the ruses she had resorted to herself when as a new bride she had wanted to meet her husband in secret, she exercised great vigilance to stop the young people from doing the same things. Of course, where Avuda was concerned, all this was totally unnecessary. He was still a boy, immersed in his activities, as yet untouched by the heady stirrings of passion. Soon after their marriage, he had spoken to Anna a few times, in the innocent companionship of youth. But he no longer did so because he was afraid of his mother.

Anna, however, was not quite as guileless as he was. She longed to talk to Avuda and sought out occasions to do so. She would steal up to him while he was at work in the field, and, if there was no one around, she would jab provocatively at his smooth hairless cheek with her finger. Avuda never quite knew what it all meant, but Anna was perfectly aware of what she was doing.

"Why are you poking my cheek?" he would turn and ask innocently. "Is it a jackfruit or a mango that you must prod to find out whether it is ripe?"

"Oh, I just did it for fun," she would reply, turning her eyes down, and smiling as she walked off.

Having worked very hard all day, digging and turning the earth, Avuda would come back at dusk, devour whatever his mother served him, curl up on his mat, and begin to snore. And what of Anna, in her corner of the kitchen? She would lie awake, tossing and turning, watching the slivers of moonlight that broke through the crevices in the wall.

Thus the days went by. Soon, it was Christmas. It was

the grandest festival of the year in their church. Both her parents-in-law were going to church. Someone had to stay home to look after the house and the many farm tools lying around in the yard. The older pair ate their dinner early, locked Anna in the house, and set out for the service at midnight.

"Avude, go to the watchman's shed and sleep there. Make sure nothing gets stolen."

All dressed up in her forty-year-old finery, the old woman walked to church. Anna could not sleep. She was still awake at midnight, pacing the little room like a caged animal. She tried each one of the locked doors, but they were too strong for her to break open. Was there no other way? She looked up, and a sudden thought struck her. Beneath the rafters, extending into the low wall, was a small crevice. She lifted herself up to it, wiggled her way through like a bandicoot, and leaped out. Her back and her elbows were grazed, but what did that matter? She stole round to the watchman's shed. There was Avuda, curled up on a torn mat near the fire pit, snoring. She stroked his back gently and said, "Imagine being so fast asleep. If a thief were to come, you'd never know."

He started awake and looked up at her.

"Who is it—you? How did you sneak out? What a fright you gave me!"

"I was scared, lying there, all alone. So I crept out through a gap in the wall," she said. "The moon is so bright tonight. Why should I lie there, suffocating, inside the house?"

"Go back and lie down. If Appan and Amma come back now, they'll kill me." Avuda was truly terrified.

"They won't be back so soon," she consoled him. "Can't you hear—the band has just begun to play?"

"If Amma feels sleepy, they'll start back early. Don't drag me into this. Just go away."

"They've gone together, haven't they? Can't the two of us be together too? Why did they get us married if we can't even talk to each other?"

She smiled meaningfully at him.

"You can talk all you want. It's me they'll beat up when Amma gets back. Go back in and lie down. Don't bother me like this."

It was a rough response and it hurt the young girl deeply. As she walked back disconsolately in the moonlight, her face grew serious with the weight of a grave decision. Avuda knew nothing of this. Indifferent as always, he had lain down on his torn mat and fallen sound asleep.

When the mother-in-law returned early the next morning, Anna was nowhere to be found. All the locks were in place.

"What can it mean? Where is she? Could she have been spirited away by some demon? Avude, did you see her last night?"

"How could I have seen her? I was outside." He drew himself up to his full length to emphasize his innocence.

"Amazing. How did she manage to get out of a locked room?"

They searched everywhere for Anna, and found her at last in her father's house, seventeen miles away. She had arrived there at daybreak.

"We don't want such a willful, undisciplined girl in

our family. Avuda will not miss her," her father-in-law shouted as he turned back, furious.

Two years passed. Avuda was no longer the same person. He had grown taller and stronger. Weeds began to take root in his mind, like the black stubble sprouting on his chin. For some inexplicable reason, he had begun to think more and more of Anna. Suddenly, it seemed, he was impatient to see her again. She must have grown. What a beautiful woman she must be now. What if he went to see her?

He said to his mother one day, as she worked hard in the kitchen, "Why don't we get her back, Amme? Things would be easier for you."

"No, no, I don't want her, or any other girl. As long as I'm alive, you'll not bring back a girl who left all by herself, and that too, at the dead of night. I can see what you're after, you rascal."

He did not pursue the matter and his mother continued to slave over the housework.

Christmas came round again. Avuda lay alone in the watchman's shed. The tapioca and climbing yams lay bathed in the pearly white moonlight. The scent of mango blossoms wafted on the soft breeze. A koel perched on a mango branch sang "kuhu-kuhu" to its mate. The happy sounds of Thiruvathira dancing flowed out of the neighboring houses. The very air seemed intoxicated, as if nature itself thrilled to the coming of the loveliest season, spring.

Avuda rose. There was a deep ache in him, as though he had lost something. What was it? His mind turned to that night two years ago. He remembered how she had come to him, and how hard it had been for her to do so. And he had simply turned her away! He was just beginning to understand. He stood in the yard uneasily, wondering what to do. It was midnight. The moon was high in the sky, but a veil of mist blurred its radiance.

Coward that he was, he first armed himself with a stick. Then he walked on fearlessly. He arrived at Anna's house at daybreak, at the very same hour that she had got there, two years ago. Her parents were taken aback. Clearly, he had not had a thought for her all this time, yet here he was, on the doorstep, impatient to see her. How strange it was. They concealed their surprise, however.

Throughout the next day, he waited for an opportunity to be alone with Anna but managed it only by dusk, when he found her watering the vegetables. She bent her head when she saw him and hid her face behind the water pot. A reproachful sigh escaped her.

"Anna, have you forgotten me?" he asked sadly. "I made a terrible mistake. I was such a child then, and so ignorant. We must never part again. I'm going to build my own house!" He confessed his guilt and comforted her, all in the same breath. Anna's eyes filled. This happiness was so unexpected. "Are you crying? What did I say to make you cry? Don't, please don't. I can't bear it."

A snake gourd that she had just watered raised its head, moist and fresh, the glare of the afternoon sun forgotten. It put out a new tendril that curled tenderly onto the bower above.

translated from Malayalam by Gita Krishnankutty

Halfway Animals

by Githa Hariharan

MY FATHER lived by the one great discovery he had made. His discovery was only a motto, and it may not seem like much to some people, but it was the one certainty he had seen proven in his life.

My father was a man of habit. Every time I visited him, even in the last years—when he was an old bag of bones heaped on a filthy bed—he greeted me in the same way.

"How is the work going, boy? Remember, Work is Worship!" He had been telling me that for more than

GITHA HARIHARAN (1954–) is one of India's most distinctive practitioners of fiction in English. Among her best-known novels are *The Thousand Faces of Night* and *The Ghosts of Vasu Master*. This piece, taken from her book *The Art of Dying and Other Stories*, is forged from an unusual combination of redundancy, stoicism, and Darwinism. It might also be considered an acknowledgement of the status of monkeys in the Indian imagination. Incidentally, in 1999 Hariharan won a famous court case that gave her the right to name her children after herself instead of carrying the father's name.

forty years, but like a compulsory ritual we would play it out each time.

He would say it in a hushed tone, his watery, yellowing eyes quickly looking to either side for eavesdroppers. I would nod obediently, and take the sum total of his life-savings carefully into my hands.

My father, it goes without saying, worked hard all his life. He really did, I think, worship the few acres of fertile land he had. He did not waste an inch of it: every patch was lovingly cultivated, tended, and harvested. A careful man, he even saved a little to buy me my first ticket to the big city.

For some reason I always thought of my father and his fields when I sat in the boss's cabin, taking down his letters. I had worked there for years, so he should have, by then, known my name. But I always overheard him say to the peon, "Call in my stenographer."

The stenographer is a peculiar kind of animal that does not hunt. It lies in wait for a more strong-hearted animal to come by and find its prey.

But this I discovered much later, as you will see. Then, I would shuffle in and sit down after a few minutes, when he indicated the chair before his desk. When he picked up his red and black striped pencil, I knew he was ready. I would open my pad, test the ink in my pen, and wait.

The pencil went into his ear and turned round and round. His eyes would fix on one spot in the room, and in this moment of concentration, the words would flow:

Dear Mr. Gupta, I am in receipt of your letter No. MG231 d. 23/2/89. I am deeply concerned that you have not yet received your order of 5000 plastic-coated sheets, as per your letter of 6/10/88.

My pen flew over the pad, leaving me behind. It made its strange squiggles quickly, one after the other, racing to keep up with him.

Then he would suddenly stop. It was at this point that I often thought of my gaunt old father solemnly looking around his fields. The pencil would come out of the boss's ear. He would take a quick whiff at it, like a hound on a trail of scent, and put it back in the other ear.

It is hard to worship an earwax addict. And all that is behind me now, so there is no need to go over a tired old story.

But I still believe, like my father, in the sanctity of work. Or habit. I get up at the same time, my heart palpitating just a little faster as the alarm goes off.

I find that my arms and legs move a little slower, shaving, taking my turn at the bathroom, and dressing. But luckily my wife, the sharp kind who is ready to pounce, has not yet noticed.

On the street, my office lunch box in my orange plastic bag, I feel protected, almost blessed. I sometimes feel, as I walk to the bus stop, a sneaky grin of glee twitching at the corners of my lips.

When my wife loses her temper, she can be quite spectacular. I often play a little game as I head for the zoo. Would she, if she found out, tear out her hair first or hit her head against the wall? Would she curse my forefathers or hers? Or would she go into one of her iron-door, month-long sulks?

I have trouble playing the same game with my son. He is our only child, but he locks himself up and studies all evening, shutting out a loving, ambitious mother and a loving, shuffling father.

The first few weeks I went to a park near the office. I read my newspaper carefully, not leaving out a single word. It's amazing how much happens to some people. I don't mean the front-page news about leaders and countries and superpowers. It's the others I am talking about. So many of them seem to get run over, burnt, raped, jailed, and shot, it's a wonder there are still some of us left.

I would read the paper all morning, but the afternoons were difficult. I would sit on a bench, under a tree if possible, and dream. But they were boring, empty dreams. It's too late to learn imagination.

Then I found the zoo. It was convenient, it opened the same hour as the office, and there were not too many people on most weekdays. I had my newspaper, and when that was finished, I could watch the animals.

I still thought of them as animals then. That was before I became an eager student. It was the gharial that first initiated me as a disciple.

I would sit on the bench by its enclosure and watch. It watched, still as a scaly rock. I waited, the newspaper forgotten, for it to move. It waited by the pool, sublimely patient, for small, unsuspecting animals to come and quench their thirst. Only its unblinking eye was alive and alert. Even if the sun shone on its still, sleeping body, the eye watched. The animals never came, but it watched and waited.

I must have spent several days by the gharial. I found

that I too could sit still, without fidgeting once, for hours. If a big, noisy group of children came up to the enclosure, I would stare at them, an endless, warning, crocodile-stare. Soon they would move on, their shrieks of excitement now hushed and muted.

But once I discovered the three enclosures of apes and monkeys, I rarely visited the companions of my early zoo days. I no longer found time to do my daily rounds of the elephants, the bears, the camels in a familiar sulk, or even the gharial.

I left the zoo early one day to find one of those small, second-hand bookshops. I found what I needed—a dog-eared, tattered copy of a book called, simply, *Primates*. The ink stamp on the first page said "New Era School," and below, in a spidery handwriting, someone had written: Not to be taken out of the library.

I now spend all day watching the apes, and reading in between. I hide the book in the hollow of the same tree every evening. I find myself looking at my wife and son with rested, almost new, eyes. I don't do too much of this, because my days are busy and eventful, and I fall asleep early every night. I sleep a deep, dreamless sleep.

Sitting at my post in front of the chimpanzee enclosure, I re-read the pages I have marked with red ink.

The idea that animals change slowly from one kind to another, I read, is called evolution. This has been going on for millions of years.

Until 1858, most people believed that life did not change. Lions always remained lions, roses never changed, humans were created as humans, and so on.

Then Charles Darwin (1809–82) and Alfred Russel

Wallace (1823–1913) proposed the idea that life did change, that it "evolved." As long as an animal fitted into its surroundings, like a worm in the ground, a fish in water, or a monkey up a tree, it would survive. But surroundings change constantly. To live successfully in an everchanging world, life itself must change as well.

"The stenographer," my boss had said the last day, "must adapt himself to change. Your old pen is no longer relevant. You can get a dictaphone or a computer. And till you can afford one, you get a stenographer who works as fast as one."

Primates, I read, are the most highly evolved animals. From the smallest to the largest, they all have something in common. Their forelimbs are fashioned into hands to hold and pick up things, and to grip branches. The four groups of primates are lemurs, monkeys, apes, and man.

When my father was dying, he could not speak. His hands gripped mine as if he did not know that hollow branches give way with even the frailest weight on them.

The night I came back with his ashes and bones—the bones, intact and unburnt—my wife gently took the urn from my hands. I never asked her what she did with it, then or later. Neither of us could speak or look each other in the eye, but in our bed that night, her hand groped across the darkness, searching for mine.

Apes are man's nearest cousins. Like us they have no tail, and can stand upright, although normally they walk about on all fours. The largest ape is the gorilla, a shy animal that roams the African jungles in small family parties.

The gorilla I see every day is sickly and lonely, not shy.

It is taken away to the zoo clinic every few weeks. It comes back some days later, looking more morose than ever. But it also has a fearsome temper. Once I saw it aim a large stone at a man who made jabbering noises at it. The stone missed, and the terrified man ran away.

Next to the gorilla is a pair of orangutans. Maybe they are happier because they have each other, or they are really the wise old men they look like. They sit all day, facing each other. Their meek, gentle heads are bowed in thought, their chins buried in their furry chests.

The chimpanzee, I read, is perhaps most like man in his body and brain. Intelligent and friendly, chimpanzees are popular with people because they perform man-like acts in zoos to win applause. They are truly nature's clowns.

The chimpanzee I watch is no clown. He is, I suppose, quite ugly, the kind of ugliness people laugh at as if they have nothing to do with it. There are three chimps in the enclosure—a male, a female, and a child.

The female chimp never sits still. She prances about, half upright, her arms hanging loosely in front of her. When she holds her baby, or when she cleans his hair all afternoon, her face is tender. She purses her thick lips as if she is humming to herself.

The male watches. He sits on a leafless pretend-tree like a sentry, always gazing outward. He sits gingerly on the branch. His bottom is a fleshy pale-pink and a protrusion, about the size of a large, hairless coconut, hangs below. Passersby notice this first. A few are shocked and quickly look away, especially if the baby chimp is playing with its mother. But most of them, especially the younger men, break into uncontrollable giggles. They nudge each other and point their fingers at his bottom. They grin knowingly or make lewd faces; some catcall. Others cup their hands over their mouths and make loud kissing and sucking noises.

The chimp watches them for a minute or two, then looks away. He continues to gaze at something beyond the enclosure. The romeos are disappointed. What's the use of that bulge, they guffaw to each other, if he won't do anything?

That evening I take my wife out for a walk. We go into a shop, not the kind in the crowded market where we usually buy our groceries and vegetables. I see her looking at a length of pale, onion-coloured silk. I tell the shopkeeper to cut a metre and pack it. She protests in whispers, but I can see she is almost smiling. I hold her fat, soft body close to mine that night. I can feel her surprise, and later her heavy, sleeping body against me.

Then one morning, the baby chimp stops clowning. It lies in a corner of the enclosure, whimpering every now and then. The mother chatters over it, and tries to make it sit upright. In between her attempts she runs round and round the enclosure in agitated circles. The male sits on his branch, gingerly as always, watching.

Later, in the afternoon, two men from the clinic come to the enclosure. The mother does not let them anywhere near the small chimp. Finally, one of them goes away and comes back with a long, sleek rifle.

I brace myself for the sound of firing, but I hear nothing. The next moment, the mother chimp screeches and screeches, jumping up and down. Soon she lies still and they take away the baby.

I have to force myself to go home in the evening. My office hours stretch beyond the stenographer's 5 p.m.

The mother chimp has been revived the next day. She seems unhurt, but she is still very agitated, because she has woken up to find that the small chimp is not in the enclosure. She jabbers and chatters, she covers her face with her arms. Her furry shoulders sag with grief.

Then, when I had almost forgotten his watchful eye, the male slowly makes his way down from his perch. He moves slowly, like a man in great pain. He lumbers up to her, making soothing, grunting noises. His face, when he turns it in the direction of my bench, is patient and dignified.

I decide to leave the zoo though I have not put in a full day. I leave earlier than usual, having received my forefather's legacy a second time around. Even unemployed, redundant stenographers know when it is time to go back to work.

Glossary

Achchi gend, middle aur off stump ke oopar: (Cricket terminology)
"A good ball on middle and off stump"

almirah: a steel cupboard

Amma: mother (in Malayali and other Indian languages of the south)

Amrutanjan: an Indian brand of balm used to relieve headaches

Appan: father (in Malayali)

Arre: a common Indian epithet indicating agitation

anna: a coin worth 1/16th of a rupee, now no longer in circulation

aswatha tree: Peepal tree, considered by Hindus the most important of trees

avatar: incarnation

babu: term of respect or endearment for a male

Baisakha: one of the months of the Hindu calendar, covering the hot summer of April-May

Bhadelo: nickname given to men who neglect their homes and travel all year round

Bhagwan: god

banian: a thin cotton vest, either worn under a shirt or by itself

bas: enough (Hindi)

bati: a unit of land area in Oriya, measuring about 20 acres

ber: a sperm whale

betel: the leaves of this plant are chewed for their medicinal qualities

bhai: brother

bhaji: a vegetable fritter

bhenchod: sisterfucker

bhidu: dude (Mumbai slang)

bidi: a cheroot (a cigar cut square at both ends)

Bombay Duck: a marine lizardfish that is dried and eaten as a delicacy

bonnet: hood

Brahman, Brahmin: the priestly caste, and so the highest and most exclusive caste in the Hindu social order (Brahmins observe many food restrictions.)

Calmpose: a sedative often used by drug addicts as a substitute

cantonment: military quarters

caravanserai: a roadside inn where travelers could rest and recover from the day's journey

Chachu, Mamu, and Bhai: terms for "uncle" and "brother," used in close friendships

chaiwalla: a tea vendor

charas: hashish

cheez: thing

chowkidar: a gateman caretaker

chulha: a stove that uses wood or charcoal as fuel

chut: slang for the genitals

dervatu: a Gujarati ceremony for marrying a widow to her brother-in-law

dholak: a barrel-shaped hand drum, often slung around the neck and played

djinni: a genie

feni: a Goan alcoholic brew made from cashew fruit

gadda: mattress

ga-le: a skirt worn by women in Arunachal Pradesh

Ganapati: an Indian god with the head of an elephant (see cover) After the festival in his name, Ganapati idols are immersed in the sea.

gharial: an Indian crocodilian with a very long snout

ghat: a series of steps leading down to a body of water such as a
river or a pond

ghoda: literally, a horse, but gangster slang for a gun

gotipuas: literally, one boy, a version of Odissi, an Oriya dance
form, performed by boys dressed as girls

gur: jaggery (see below)

haan: yes (Hindi)

Hanuman: A monkey-god of great powers, and Rama's most
trusted ally in the Ramayana

Harijan: a term referring to Dalits or the lowest in the Hindu
caste order, once shunned as untouchables

hijras: eunuchs

hillstation: a high-altitude city or town, usually patronized by
tourists

Jains: those who follow Jainism, an ancient dharmic religion that
prescribes non-violence for all forms of living beings

ji: suffix used with a name or title to show respect

jaggery: unrefined brown sugar made from palm sap

jilebi: a deep-fried sweet (A jilebi hero might be thought of as
having "chocolate-boy" looks.)

Kapil Dev: a famous Indian cricketer

Kartak (Kartik): one of the names of the months in the Hindu
calendar, corresponding to October-November of the
Gregorian system

khallasi: sailor

kirtan: religious singing

koel: an Indian cuckoo, much celebrated in Indian life and
literature for its sweet voice

kabaddi: a popular game in India, played in a field by two teams
of players who raid each other's halves

khabari: informant

khichri: an Indian meal made of rice and lentils cooked together,
often eaten with ghee (clarified butter) and yoghurt

kunukku: an earring worn by Keralite Christians, consisting of a
thin circular chain with a small ball hanging from it

kurta: a long, loose shirt-like garment worn on the upper body, usually over loose pyjamas

Lakshmi: the Indian goddess of wealth

level-crossings: railroad crossings

lingam: a cylinder-shaped stone that is a symbol for the worship of the Hindu deity Shiva

lorries: trucks

lungi: a long piece of cloth wrapped around the lower half of the body, worn by men

maderchod: motherfucker

maharani: the wife of a maharaja, or a princess

malai: cream

Marshman and Tod: John Clark Marshman and James Tod, 19th-century British writers of books on India

matric (short for matriculation): a term commonly used to refer to the final year of high school

maikukal: a local version of biryani, or rice cooked with meat and spices

maulvi: a Muslim religious cleric or teacher

mehendi: henna patterns applied to a woman's hands and feet at her wedding

mekhela: the bottom portion of a traditional woman's garment in Assam, draped from the waist downwards

memsaab: rich or classy woman (Hindi)

Mere desh ki dharti sona ugle, ugle heere moti: A line from a famous Hindi film song, eulogising the country (desh) and its fertile earth (dharti) that sprouts gold and precious stones

miglun: foreigner (Arunachali)

mithun: a domesticated bovine found in the northeast, often sacrificed for important occasions and indicating the relative prosperity of the sacrificer

neera: the sweet translucent sap from the palm tree, widely drunk in India

paan, or pan: betel leaf rolled up with areca nut and lime, commonly chewed both as a palate cleanser and after meals *paani:* water (Hindi)

panchayat: traditional village council of five wise, respected elders chosen by the community ("Panch" means "five" in Hindi.) Today panchayats are elected by the village community through voting.

Partition, partition riots: Colonial India was partitioned into the two states of India and Pakistan when the British ceded independence in 1947, resulting in one of the largest migrations of human beings in history. Many Indian Muslims chose to move to Pakistan; similarly, many Hindus in Pakistan migrated to India. Widespread religious violence was a distressing feature of Partition, and has become part of the cultural memory of both nations.

phataak memsaab: "Memsaab" is a rich or classy woman; "phataak" is Mumbai slang that means something like "sensational"

pir: a Muslim mystic

ponung girls: adolescent girls

portugis: a person from Portugal

Poush: A month in the Hindu calendar corresponding to December-January

prasad: food made holy by being first offered to the gods

pucca: literally, sure, used to indicate a concrete (proper) building or road rather than a makeshift one

purdah: literally, curtain, the practice of women covering their faces when outside so as not to be seen by men

putalvel: a ceremony performed when a fisherman is believed to be dead but his body is not found

raja: king

Ramnavami: a widely celebrated festival celebrating the birth of Lord Ram, the hero of the *Ramayana*

randi: prostitute

rangoli: an art form in which coloured powders make patterns on the thresholds of houses on festival days

rauza: mausoleum

rebab: a small wooden stringed instrument commonly found in Persian music

rotla: traditional millet flour bread

rudra veena: a stringed instrument with two bowls made of gourds

saadi, satrangi: types of country liquor

salaam: to greet; a greeting

samaan: goods (Hindi); gun (gangster slang)

Sangeet Mahavidyalaya: school of music

saragwa: drumstick tree

shikara: a wooden tarpaulin-covered boat native to Kashmir

Solung: a week-long religious festival observed by the Adi tribe of Arunachal Pradesh, featuring rites connected to agriculture and the sacrifice of animals, such as pigs and mithun (Indian bison)

tangdi: chicken leg

tantrik: a man of god who claims knowledge of the occult

tava: an iron griddle used for making Indian flatbreads

thali: plate

Thiruvathira: a Malayali festival celebrated by women singing and dancing

Tulsidas: a 16th-century poet, philosopher, and composer of the Ramacharitamanas, a colloquial version of the Ramayana that is still widely read in Hindu households in north India

torch: flashlight

tura: a kind of eel

urs: death anniversary

vade/vada: a vegetarian deep-fried snack commonly sold in street stalls and railway stations

wah: an exclamation signifying great pleasure or delight, like "Wow"

yaara: buddy

zamindar: a holder or occupier of land, a feudal overlord

Zil-Qa'da: the eleventh month of the Islamic calendar, falling in the sacred time of Hajj

PERMISSIONS

Salman Rushdie's "The Prophet's Hair" from *East, West: Stories*, © 1994 by Salman Rushdie, published by Pantheon Books, USA, and Jonathan Cape, UK. Reprinted by permission of Pantheon Books, a division of Random House, Inc., and by The Random House Group Ltd., UK.

Qurratulain Hyder's "The Sound of Falling Leaves," translated by Carla Petievich, from *Modern Indian Literature: An Anthology*, Volume 2, edited by KM George, Sahitya Akademi, New Delhi, 1993. English © 1993 Carla Petievich. Reprinted by permission of the Sahitya Akademi.

Kunal Basu's "The Accountant," from *The Japanese Wife* (HarperCollins, New Delhi, 2007). © 2007 Kunal Basu. Reprinted by permission of the Capel & Land Agency, on behalf of the author.

Mamang Dai's "The Scent of Orange Blossom," from *Legends of Pensam* (Penguin, New Delhi, 2006)

Phanishwarnath Renu's "Panchlight," from *The Third Vow and Other Stories* by Phanishwarnath Renu, translated by Kathryn G. Hansen (Chanakya Publications, New Delhi, 1986). English © Kathryn G. Hansen. Reprinted by permission of the translator.

Bibhutibhushan Bandhopadhyay's "Canvasser Krishnalal," from *A Strange Attachment and Other Stories*, translated by Phyllis Granoff, (Mosaic Press, Oakville, Ontario). Reprinted by permission of the translator.

Fakir Mohan Senapati's "Asura Pond," translated by Rabi Shankar Mishra, Satya P. Mohanty, Jatindra K. Nayak, and Paul St. Pierre, from *Six Acres and a Third* (© 2005 University of California Press). Reprinted by permission of the University of California Press. Originally published in 1901.

Nazir Mansuri's "The Whale," translated by Nikhil Khandekar, from *Katha Prize Stories Volume 7*, edited by Geeta Dharmarajan and Meenakshi Sharma (Katha, New Delhi, 1998). Reprinted by permission of Katha Books.

Vikram Chandra's "Ganesh Gaitonde Sells his Gold," from *Sacred Games* (HarperCollins, USA and Faber & Faber Ltd, UK, 2007). © 2007 Vikram Chandra. Reprinted by permission of HarperCollins Publishers and Faber and Faber, Ltd.

233

CHANDRAHAS CHOUDHURY is a novelist and literary critic based in Mumbai (Bombay). His first novel, *Arzee the Dwarf,* appeared in India in 2009, and was shortlisted for the Commonwealth First Book Award. He is the book critic of the Indian newspaper *Mint Lounge,* and his essays and reviews have also appeared in *Foreign Policy,* the *Washington Post,* the *Los Angeles Times,* and the *San Francisco Chronicle.* He also writes the widely read literary weblog The Middle Stage.

ANITA DESAI is the John E. Burchard Professor of Writing at Massachusetts Institute of Technology, and a Fellow of the American Academy of Arts and Letters. One of India's most widely admired novelists, she is the author of more than a dozen acclaimed works of fiction, including *Fire on the Mountain* (1977), *Village by the Sea* (1982), *In Custody* (1984), *Journey to Ithaca* (1995), and *Fasting, Feasting* (1999)